CHRISTIAN THE LION

THE ILLUSTRATED LEGACY

CHRISTIAN THE LION

THE ILLUSTRATED LEGACY

JOHN RENDALL

with photographs by DEREK CATTANI

Bradt

For Tallulah, Max and Nicky Rendall, and Katrina and Adam Cattani

IN MEMORY OF ANN CATTANI

First published in October 2018 by
Bradt Travel Guides Ltd
IDC House, The Vale, Chalfont St Peter, Bucks SL9 9RZ, England
www.bradtguides.com

Print edition published in the USA by The Globe Pequot Press Inc,
PO Box 480, Guilford, Connecticut 06437-0480

Text copyright © 2018 John Rendall
Photographs copyright © 2018 Derek Cattani
Additional photographs © as credited beside each image.
Images by Tony Fitzjohn © George Adamson Wildlife Preservation Trust (GAWPT)
Edited by Mike Unwin
Proofread by Shermila Valentine
Cover design and design development by Richard Czapnik
Layout and typesetting by Namrita Price-Goodfellow, D & N Publishing
Maps by David McCutcheon FBCart.S
Front cover photograph by Derek Cattani
Back cover photograph by Simon Trevor
Production managed by Sue Cooper, Bradt & Jellyfish Print Solutions

ISBN: 978 1 78477 621 3 (print pb)
           978 1 78477 639 8 (print hb)
e-ISBN: 978 1 78477 561 2 (e-pub)
e-ISBN: 978 1 78477 462 2 (mobi)

British Library Cataloguing in Publication Data
A catalogue record for this book is available from the British Library

Digital conversion by www.dataworks.co.in
Printed in India

CONTENTS

PREFACE

In 1969, Harrods luxury department store in London sold a three-month-old lion cub to two young Australians, John Rendall and Anthony (Ace) Bourke. They named him Christian.

For a year, Christian lived happily with John and Ace and his human pride. His home was a pine furniture shop called Sophistocat in the World's End on Chelsea's King's Road. It was here that Fleet Street photographer Derek Cattani first began photographing him.

When Christian outgrew London, he was entrusted to the care of George Adamson in Kenya. He and his wife Joy had already successfully rehabilitated a lioness named Elsa, a story known to the world through Joy's book *Born Free* and the film of the same name.

In 1971, one year after Christian had started living in the wild, John and Ace returned to Kenya in an attempt to find him and see how he was adapting.

The film clip of their emotional reunion has now been viewed by over 100 million people on YouTube.

In 1972, John and Ace returned for a second reunion. Christian, although still affectionate, was much more mature and now preoccupied with wild lionesses. George's rehabilitation programme was succeeding.

In 1973, Christian disappeared into the wild forever. But George heard him mating and was confident that Christian had established his own pride. George Adamson had succeeded in rehabilitating a fifth-generation zoo-bred lion in the wild. It was the first time this had ever been done.

When John and Ace took Christian to Kenya in 1970, there were an estimated 400,00 lions in Africa. Today there are fewer than 20,000. The future of Christian's descendants is as precarious as that of rhino and the elephant – and, in fact, of all Africa's wildlife.

HOW I MET CHRISTIAN

In the 60s and 70s, The King's Road in Chelsea was a mecca for fascinating people and party invitations, and it was at a Chelsea party that I first met John and Ace. I was then a young freelance Fleet Street photographer, always on the hunt for an interesting picture story. When I heard about the two men buying a lion from Harrods and taking it for walks down the King's Road, I just knew I had to meet this lion cub.

A few days later John and Ace invited me to Sophistocat pine furniture shop in the World's End to meet Christian. He was then a three-month-old cuddly cub, with sharp teeth and the most amazing eyes. I realised that I would have to get to know this beautiful little animal if I was to get good photographs. Instead of grabbing my camera and shooting away, I just sat on the floor watching him, and waited.

Eventually, curiosity overcame him and Christian inched his way towards me and then pushed his head against mine. John explained that this was a sure sign of welcome. Over the following weeks I made regular visits, slowly gaining Christian's trust and John and Ace's approval of my patient attitude. They saw that I was not just after a snarling one-off picture for a feature, and offered me the job as Christian's official photographer.

Christian soon accepted me as one of his human pride. To him, my camera became a natural extension of my arm and not something to worry about – or chew. Soon I was able to spend long periods of time with him, and he would just ignore the fact that I was capturing him on film. Some of my favourite moments with Christian were of him in John and Ace's flat: surely a unique location in which to photograph any lion.

As Christian grew bigger, so did the cost of his meals. To generate some income, John, Ace and I came up with a few fun picture stories that we could sell to the now eager Fleet Street press. The Easter chicks feature (see pages 52–3) was published in all but a couple of the national tabloids. We never pushed Christian to do anything he didn't naturally want to do, however. Playing with a football in Moravian Close was a favourite pastime, as were fun car journeys down the King's Road. His gentle nature allowed him to be with children and friends alike.

It was my good fortune to be invited to travel with John, Ace and the film crew to document the first stage of Christian's rehabilitation with George Adamson in Kenya. As part of his London pride, we all took comfort from being together in such a strange and exciting land. Knowing Christian has left me with a lifelong love of animals and a special appreciation for the beauty of the wild lion that he was to become.

I dedicate my part in this book to my wonderful late wife Ann. Her tireless help and support played a large part in many of Christian's photo sessions. She, too, was one of Christian's human pride.

Derek Cattani, 2018

CHRISTIAN'S MONUMENT

In ancient Egypt, a pyramid was both a tomb and a monument. But I didn't look on the new reserve at Kora as Christian's graveyard. For one thing, he was only four years old, and a lion can live for twelve or fifteen years in the wild. For another, he had blazed a trail across the Tana to the great open hunting ground in the north, and I liked to imagine him exploring its opportunities for new life.

It would therefore be premature and pessimistic to think of the cheerful, mischievous and courageous young lion from London as dust 'in that rich earth concealed; a dust that England bore'.

On the other hand, I did begin to think of Kora as Christian's monument. And this has often put strength into my fight to protect it as a place where life can continue as it has done for millennia, before it was threatened with dissolution by pressures let loose from other continents in the last fifty years.

George Adamson
From *My Pride and Joy: An Autobiography*
first published Simon and Schuster 1987

1

FROM ILFRACOMBE ZOO TO HARRODS

The lion cub destined to be called Christian was born, appropriately, on the cusp of the sign of Leo, during the second or third week of August 1969. He was one of four cubs born to Butch and Mary, two captive lions in a small country zoo high above the picturesque coastal village of Ilfracombe in Devon.

Christian at three months old

Life in the wild is tough for lion cubs. Predators such as leopard and hyena are always ready to snatch an unguarded infant, while a new alpha male taking over a pride often kills any existing youngsters in order to replace them with his own genetic lineage. Furthermore, the cubs always eat last at a kill and thus in drought years are first to suffer. Even in good times, only a third of all cubs survive to the age of two.

Born in Devon, Christian was spared the harsh realities of life in the wild. Nonetheless, life in a zoo also has its perils. Captive lionesses may neglect their cubs, or be too inexperienced to raise them successfully in the unnatural environment of a zoo. For their own safety, cubs are often removed from their mothers. So it was with Christian and his sisters.

Ilfracombe Zoo had no room for more lions, so the cubs were taken from their parents to be hand-reared by zoo staff, kept warm under a radiator in a staff flat. Even before the cubs opened their eyes the surrogate parents noted that one was calmer than the other three. At three months old, two of the females were sold to an animal dealer and then, reputedly, to a circus. The two remaining cubs, by then named Marcus and Martha, were sent for resale to Harrods department store in Knightsbridge, London. Marcus was the calm one. Nobody could have predicted his future.

Six months after we had bought Christian from Harrods, Ace and I visited Ilfracombe Zoo to see Christian's parents, Butch and Mary. They were

Mary, Christian's mother, at Ilfracombe Zoo JOHN RENDALL

magnificent animals, but living in a distressingly small cement-and-wire compound, around which they endlessly paced. It was immediately apparent that Christian had inherited his parent's strong genes and would one day grow a mane just as impressive as his father's. We visited incognito, and to this day I regret not having introduced ourselves and perhaps finding out more about Christian's parents. The zoo belonged to Charles Trevisick, who had bred many lions there – including, apparently, 53 from one pair he had owned before Butch and Mary – all of whom had been sold into the exotic animal market of zoos and circuses. How lucky was Christian to escape this fate!

What history we did know about Christian's background had come from the information supplied to Harrods. Butch had come from the Jerusalem Biblical Zoo in Israel, founded in 1940 to provide research facilities for students studying animals mentioned in *The Bible*. I have been unable to find any records of his birth or the details of his journey to Ilfracombe, but Butch must have been 6 or 7 years old in 1970 and probably weighed over 500lbs; a lion in his prime.

Mary had come from the Royal Rotterdam Zoo in Holland. Intriguingly, this was also where Elsa's two sisters, Big One and Lustica, had been sent after they were taken from George and Joy Adamson in late

Butch, Christian's father, at Ilfracombe Zoo JOHN RENDALL

1956 – the Kenya Game Department having decided that the couple could keep only one of the cubs that George had saved after he shot their stock-killing mother. George thus always wondered whether Christian might be related to Elsa. No stud books were kept in those days – or if they were, they are now untraceable – so it has never been possible to confirm any relationship between Christian and Elsa. Nonetheless, George enjoyed the fantasy that the two lions might have shared genes.

Christian had been described by Harrods as a 'fifth generation zoo-bred lion'. With no records to confirm this, it was a word-of-mouth pedigree. What was indisputable, however, was that neither of his parents had ever roamed the plains of Africa. By the time we visited Ilfracombe Zoo, Christian was already nine months old. Seeing his two beautiful parents in such a confined space served to strengthen our resolve that he would not be spending his life in a zoo.

Harrods, Knightsbridge, 1969
COURTESY OF HARRODS COMPANY ARCHIVE, LONDON

PETS AT CHRISTMAS

Thinking of buying pets as Christmas presents? MR. R. HAZLE (Buyer of Harrods Zoo) provides some hints.

Marcus and Marta, the two lion cubs who have taken over our Zoo, are proving a great attraction. Two months old when they came to us from a Devon zoo, they have settled down very well. It will no doubt be a difficult task to find a home for them where they will be completely happy, but, as in the case of our pumas, we feel confident it will work out well. Visitors are not readily convinced that these appealing, floppy, furry creatures grow into animals requiring an increasing amount of time and affection to maintain the feeling of security so essential to any 'tame wild animal.' Domestic kittens are obviously a wiser choice for Christmas presents, together with puppies, guinea pigs, hamsters, budgerigars, etc. But we in the Pet Shop believe it is not altogether wise to have a new pet in the house at Christmas. It is often better to promise an animal or bird but to have it in the home after the Christmas festivities, when affection can be concentrated on it and the new pet made to feel completely at home.

A pet that would be absolutely at ease at Christmas, however is at the other end of the scale from Marcus and Marta—the active and inquisitive gerbil. The size of a hamster, needing just as little space and similar feeding, this little rodent is fast becoming the favourite pet for children of all ages. It hardly ever bites—unless handled roughly—and is normally busy all day providing entertainment by its antics and its air of almost frenzied activity. Even when apparently asleep, it will spring to life and proceed to investigate the cause. They are often kept in pairs but then show a marked inclination to multiply,

A mirror can give many hours' amusement to lion cubs. Marcus and Marta cost £250 each.

and they can build up to a thriving little colony fairly quickly. But it is difficult to imagine a pet that would enjoy the bustle of Christmas more, and without involving the family in the confusion and minor chaos that could be caused by including Marcus or Marta among the presents under the Christmas tree.

It was not until 1976 that the Endangered Species Act (Import and Export) banned the sale of exotic animals in England. In 1969 Harrods were thus legally able to sell the cubs they had acquired from Ilfracombe Zoo.

Harrods' Zoo, located on the second floor between the music department and the carpet department, was a popular attraction in the store. Parents brought their children to see – and sometimes make a purchase from – the wide variety of domestic animals and birds displayed. Most purchases were of pedigree dogs and cats, budgerigars, canaries, parrots, guinea pigs, hamsters and the like. Occasionally, however, there was something more exotic on offer. Tapirs, snakes, monkeys, pumas and a lion cub called Justin had all previously been sold here, and the store claimed that it could provide anything for a customer.

ABOVE: **An extract from Harrods's in-house magazine depicts zoo buyer Roy Hazle with the two lion cubs, Martha and Marcus** COURTESY OF HARRODS COMPANY ARCHIVE, LONDON

Adding to the fascination for visitors were the stories of the celebrities who had bought such creatures. The actress Beatrice Lille had bought a crocodile here as a Christmas present for the playwright Noel Coward. And in 1967, when still Governor of California, Ronald Reagan had purchased an elephant called Gertie as a mascot for a Republican Party rally. An apocryphal report claimed that when the Harrods assistant received the enquiry he had asked whether Mr Reagan wanted an African or an Indian elephant.

Such were the stories circulating when I first visited the zoo with fellow Australian Ace Bourke in November 1969. Our visit was prompted by simple curiosity: we wanted to confirm a story told me by a beautiful Australian girl, Barrie Assheton-Chin. Barrie had been married to the American Ambassador in Rome, where she had been frequently painted by the celebrated artist Pietro Annigoni. Following an exhibition of Pietro's paintings in London, which included a number of portraits of Barrie, the painter had taken her to lunch at the popular San Lorenzo restaurant in Beauchamp Place and then to nearby Harrods to buy her a celebration present. They found themselves in the zoo where, in jest, Barrie had decided to test Harrods' claim that they could provide anything for their customers by asking for a camel. 'Of course, Madam,' the salesman had responded calmly. 'Would that be with one hump or two?'

Growing up in Sydney, Australia, where the most sophisticated department store was David Jones, which certainly did not have a pet department, let alone a zoo, it was hard to believe such extraordinary stories. But when I saw two lion cubs for sale in Harrods I had to accept Barrie's story about the camel. There they were: two beautiful lion cubs in a cage between the Siamese cats and Old English sheepdogs.

Ace and I sat and watched the young lions quietly. We were enthralled by their beauty but also concerned by their conditions, confined in such a small cage and exposed to so many excited and demanding people.

In fact, the cubs did not spend all day in their cage but appeared only when the assistant buyer, Sandy Lloyd, decided they were relaxed or tired enough to spend time in front of the public. At other times, they retreated to their own private space behind the public area. Sandy was even allowed take them to play on the rooftop. Ignorant of this on our first visit, however, we were determined to buy both cubs and provide them with a better place to live – not that I had any idea of where that place might be!

A sign on the cubs' cage announced that the male was called Marcus and the female Martha. It rapidly became clear that Marcus was far calmer than his sister. While she flattened her ears and hissed at the children who crowded around the cage, he simply stared through everyone, not deigning to acknowledge their presence. Although only a cub, and reminiscent of a real live teddy bear, there was something disconcerting about the self-assured expression in his eyes. It implied a strength of character that made him irresistible.

'Why don't we buy him?' I suggested. 'I've already called him Christian,' replied Ace. Marcus may have been a fine strong name for a lion but Christian was so much more evocative of the historic confrontations between Christians and lions.

It seems the decision had been made. But before going any further, there were many questions to answer and logistics to sort out. First, the cost: the cage carried nothing so vulgar as a price tag, and I struggled to keep calm when a sales assistant quoted 250 guineas (approximately £3,500 in 2018). Traditionally thoroughbred horses are sold in guineas so the implication was clear: Harrods only sold animals of pedigree, even lions. This was a considerable sum of money, given that you could buy a decent second-hand car for the same amount and rent a flat in Chelsea for £20 a week.

Also, any prospective purchaser would first have to convince Harrods that they would make suitable owners for the cubs. We arranged our first meeting with Sandy Lloyd. As assistant buyer, she spent the most time with the cubs and had a proprietorial interest in their well-being. The cubs may have been promoted as 'the Christmas present for the person who has everything,' but money alone was not going to secure their purchase. I suspected that Sandy was playing for time at this first meeting, when she patiently answered our many excited but naïve questions, but she did give us a sense of hope when she invited us to return the following day to meet the zoo buyer, Roy Hazle. He would make the final decision on the sale.

And so began a series of interviews and visits to try to convince Roy and Sandy that we would make responsible owners. Opening hours in 1969 were from 9 a.m. until 5.30 p.m., with no universal late-night or Sunday shopping. At the end of the day, when other shoppers had gone home, we would thus come to the zoo and play with the cubs in order to help us make a realistic decision about their purchase. This was a wise plan of Roy and Sandy's because it became instantly apparent that we could only cope with one cub. Even at just thirty pounds, each was more than a handful as they leapt around and wrestled with each other and with us: balls of energy with needle-sharp teeth. Martha was the more aggressive, so any thoughts of buying her were soon abandoned. Besides, the cost of buying both was way beyond our budget. Thus we focused our attention on Christian.

Roy also suggested we meet two young men, Charles Bewick and Peter Bowan, who had bought a puma from the zoo the previous year. This animal was called Margot, after Charles's friend, the prima ballerina Margot Fonteyn. She lived with them in an impressive house in Battersea where she had the run of the walled garden and an attic floor to herself. At a dinner Charles and Peter gave for Dame Margot, her mother, Mrs Hookham, was unimpressed by the cat being named in her daughter's honour and not amused by its presence at the dinner table.

Margot was a beautiful animal: svelte pale grey, with a long, elegant tail. Though suspicious of strangers, she obviously had a trusting relationship with Charles and Peter. That was encouraging, and the two explained the ramifications of living with a big cat in London: the cost, the time involved, and the numerous other problems – such as the difficulty of going away for weekends, the nervousness of guests and the concerns of neighbours.

Meeting Margot was an important part of our learning curve. It was understandable that she was not interested in having more people in her life: wild pumas are largely solitary animals and do not live in a pride, as lions do. So, although we were wary of her, we concluded, optimistically, that living with a lion – a more gregarious species – would actually be easier.

Meanwhile, a problem remained. Where would we live with Christian? By the time I arrived in England in 1969 I had exhausted the travelling funds I had saved in Australia so had to find a job as soon as possible. Barrie, our Australian friend who had been painted by Annigoni, was now living in London and kindly offered me the spare room in her Chelsea flat while I looked for work and somewhere more permanent to live. Thankfully, it was so much easier to find a job in 'swinging London' in the late 60s than it is today: you simply strolled through the door and asked for one. People came and went, without contracts, to work in restaurants, shops, antique markets, photographic studios and clubs. You just had to ask.

Around the corner from Barrie's flat was the King's Road, where two enterprising young Englishmen, Joe Harding and John Barnardiston, had opened a pine furniture shop called Sophistocat.

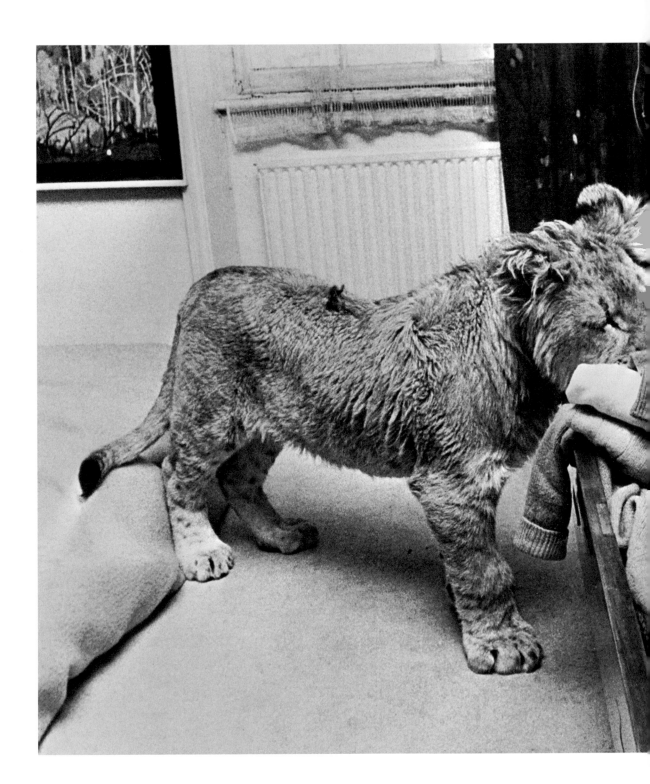

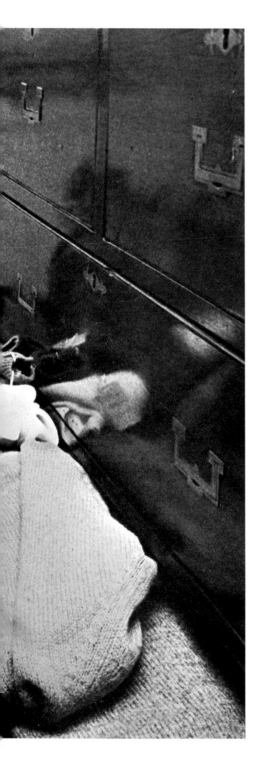

Pine furniture, once found only in children's rooms or spare bedrooms, had become a more fashionable product for the relaxed lifestyle of the 60s when, rather than entertaining in formal dining rooms, people would gather friends casually in their kitchens. Joe and John had gone skiing, so the shop manager, a glamorous ex-model named Jennifer-Mary Taylor, took me on for extra help. I knew nothing about pine furniture but assured Jennifer-Mary I could soon learn. It was exciting to be working in the King's Road, with its glamorous clientele. What's more, there was a spare room in the flat above the shop.

But where could Christian live? After some frustrating searches for suitable quarters – even placing a small ad in a local paper – we were no closer to finding him a home. The only option was to persuade Jennifer-Mary that he should come and live at Sophistocat. It was an outrageous request, but I argued that surely a lion was the ultimate 'sophistocat' and that he would thus make an appropriate mascot for the shop. With Joe and John away skiing it really was unfair to pressure Jennifer-Mary, but Joe had been born in Kenya so we considered that was tantamount to approval.

Fortunately, this presumption turned out to be correct. Joe and John agreed enthusiastically and it was decided that Christian could come and live in Sophistocat, with a floor below the shop to himself. We returned to Harrods with the good news, hoping Roy Hazle and Sandy Lloyd would approve. To our delight they did, and a date was set to collect Christian in three weeks' time. One week later, however we received a phone call: 'Can you come and collect Christian tomorrow?' It transpired that the two cubs had escaped the night before and virtually destroyed a display of goat skin carpets in the carpet department, whose manager was less than pleased. Clearly, Christian had outgrown his time at Harrods.

Christian makes himself useful in the flat
above Sophisticat

2

LION AT THE WORLD'S END

The World's End district, at the western end of Chelsea's King's Road, was an integral part of 'swinging London' in the 1960s, as well-known as Carnaby Street for its fashionable boutiques and clubs. Its raffish reputation dated back to the 17th century, when the Pheasantry, further up the road, had been built as a royal hunting lodge and to raise pheasants for the royal household. Back then the World's End had marked the end of the 'King's Road,' the place where the protection of the king ended and highwaymen reputedly lurked.

Christian attracts young admirers as he heads out in the Bentley

The Pheasantry had been saved from demolition through a campaign led by Sir John Betjamin, and by 1969 had become a restaurant and club. Its upper rooms were rented to musicians, artists and writers, including Eric Clapton and our fellow Australians Germaine Greer and Martin Sharp, the latter being the Australian artist who created Oz magazine alongside Richard Neville, Richard Walsh and Felix Dennis.

Among Sophistocat's close neighbours were Vivienne Westwood and Malcom McClaren, whose boutique, then called Seditions, later became the birthplace of the Punk movement. Opposite were John Pearse and Nigel Waymouth's Granny Takes a Trip boutique, where the Beatles, the Who, Cream and Jimmy Hendrix were all regular customers, and Gary Craze's hairdresser's, Tod's. And further up the road, towards Sloane Square, were the shops of designers Ossie Clarke and Mary Quant, and the boutiques Just Men, Tommy Robert's Mr Freedom, Skin and the Chelsea Antique Market, where Sydney fashionista Jenny Kee had a stall with Swedish beauty Ulla Laarson.

All these places were obligatory shopping destinations for the fashion-conscious and rock stars of the day. And they changed their stock every week, necessitating the weekly stroll down one side of the King's Road and back to Sloane Square on the other. Meanwhile the Rolling Stones rehearsed in the back room of the Wetherby Arms, our local pub, which was convenient for Ronnie Wood, who lived just around the corner. It was all heady stuff, and a sprinkling of Australians were only too ready to join in the excitement and energy that drew people of all nationalities and talents to London.

Perhaps, therefore, it was not totally outrageous that a lion cub should live in such a Bohemian community. At Sophistocat, on the lower floor, Christian had his own territory, with bedding, bones, favourite toys and a large litter tray, which he used

Christian prowling through Sophistocat pine furniture store

Christian with his beloved plastic toy pig

assiduously after only a few days of encouragement. There was plenty of natural light and space for him to race around in, often dragging a much favoured rolled-up mattress, and plenty of room to romp with his best friend Unity Bevis who came to visit every afternoon.

Unity was an actress who had once owned a lioness in Rome, called Lola, while working at the Cinecitta film studio with Frederico Fellini, director of such classics as *La Dolce Vita* and *Juliet of the Spirits*. Unity had acted under the stage name Anna Varezzi but Fellini had always called her 'La Gatina' (the kitten) because of Lola. The first time Unity first came to see Christian we were sceptical about her Lola stories and rather cursorily dismissed her, claiming that Christian was asleep. But, undeterred, Unity reappeared the next day and the day after that, until finally we relented.

How fortunate we were that Unity persisted. She soon became an essential part of Christian's daily routine. Her experience with Lola had taught her exactly how to handle a boisterous cub and, at just over five feet tall, she knew better than we did that physical strength was no way to contain a lion's energy. It was Unity who taught us the power of voice and behaviour. If Christian became too rough, Unity would simply stand still and ignore him. This was not always easy, as he pushed and shoved, but he soon got the message that something was wrong. Indeed, the most effective punishment was to ignore him and leave him alone in his den. Whenever Unity did this, Christian would be gentle and loving as soon as she returned. It was a technique Ace and I quickly adopted. And so a manageable routine was established, with all of Christian's friends – his new human pride – in place to care for him.

Harrods had supplied us with a detailed diet sheet for Christian's four daily meals. No wild lion cub would ever be so well fed and it was no wonder that he grew so quickly. Breakfast and tea comprised liquid meals, based on Complan or Farex (powdered milk energy drinks) mixed with milk, a raw egg and vitamins. Lunch and supper consisted of raw meat, generally chopped beef or rabbit, dusted with bone meal, a hard-boiled egg and, as a special treat, a marrow-filled bone – basically raw *ossobucco*. Feeding Christian cost us roughly £30 a week. But we had help: a kindly local chef contributed steaks from his restaurant that had passed their sell-by date, while neighbouring butchers provided cut-price marrow bones, which Christian loved.

At all meal times one of us sat with Christian and hand-fed him, so he never had any sense of competition for his food. He was unconcerned if we moved his food bowl or took a bone from him. Competition would be something Christian had to learn once he was in Africa.

Christian was never ill. He made only one visit to the vet and that was for a Katavac inoculation shot. When I rang the surgery of Kensington-based vet Keith Butt, the secretary was extremely nonchalant about bringing Christian in, saying that no special appointment was necessary. We duly turned up, and sat in reception between various cats and dogs, awaiting our turn. In the surgery Keith gave Christian an injection – at which he didn't flinch – and reassured us that he was 'a very fine and healthy chap.' Many years later, a particularly feisty Jack Russell terrier of mine called 'Digger' nipped Keith while receiving his inoculations. 'I'd rather have that lion of yours any day than this little blighter,' said Keith, nursing his finger.

Sophistocat opened at 10 a.m. By then, Christian had been fed, enjoyed his playtime in the Moravian Close (see page 39) and returned home for a nap, leaving us to get on with running the shop. By lunchtime, he would be awake and ready for that first meat meal. Then it was playtime in the den with

Unity. Christian would moan excitedly from behind the door when he heard her arrive. 'You're too close, Christian; get back,' she would say. Then, listening carefully: 'Where are you now, Christian?' A moan or grunt would tell her when he had moved away from the door, and only when she was satisfied that he would not knock her over would she enter. Once inside, he would rush across to greet her and the games would begin.

By the end of the afternoon Christian was ready for tea. He would then come up into the shop and wander happily around, eventually opting to sit on a table or chest of drawers in the window, where he had a good view of the passing shoppers and traffic. Local children would come to see him in the evenings. 'That's Christian, our World's End Lion,' they would inform unsuspecting King's Road shoppers, who stopped and stared in disbelief.

Within the first weeks of Christian's arrival at Sophistocat another neighbour entered our lives and became part of Christian's human pride: photographer Derek Cattani, whose photographs are the focus of this book. Jennifer-Mary had taken a few snaps, but neither Ace nor I had made an effort to photograph Christian's first weeks with us. Derek was a successful Fleet Street photographer from the old school, prepared for any assignment, from news stories to football matches, motor racing, showbiz portraits or royal occasions. He took photographing a lion in his stride, and offered to start a record of Christian's life. There was no need for a discussion: it was a great offer and it is thanks to Derek that we have these wonderful photographs of Christian in both London and Kenya. Christian became so used to Derek being around that he ignored the light meters and other professional paraphernalia, and even accepted Derek physically shifting him into positions for better shots.

Christian with John on the stairs at Sophistocat

Christian with John and Ace on a pine table at Sophistocat

Christian demolishing a waste paper basket

Christian had some well-known visitors from the world of show business. These included actor Corin Redgrave and actress Mia Farrow. The latter, though heavily pregnant, was not afraid of cuddling Christian – although her husband, conductor Andre Previn, opted to watch from outside the shop. Similarly, while actress Diana Rigg had no qualms, her 007 co-star in *On Her Majesty's Secret Service*, Australian George Lazenby, did not live up to his James Bond image and refused to enter the shop. Sadly, Christian was playing in the Moravian Close on the morning John Lennon bought a table, so will never know whether Christian might have inspired a Beatles song.

There were also, of course, calls from people expressing their concern about us keeping a lion. Some threatened that they would report us to the RSPCA or other authorities. We would always suggest to such individuals that they should come and visit Christian before taking things any further. At this point some just hung up, but a few did come to check us out and in every case Christian won them over. People who had initially been aggressive were instantly charmed by him. They could see how content and healthy he was, how much he loved us and how loved he was by his human pride.

Sometimes we had supper in the shop; after all, we were not short of dining tables and chairs. But Christian was uninterested in our suppers because it was time for his final meal of the day. A sleepy little lion would then follow us down to his den, where he instantly slumped onto his bedding. If we had been to the theatre or out to a party we would pop in to check on him when we returned, but he was usually in a deep sleep. Lions in the wild are primarily nocturnal but Christian had adapted to human sleeping patterns. Once, however, we found him wide awake when we came home. In his enthusiasm, he jumped up on Jennifer-Mary and snagged the straps on her new Biba ballgown. She was less than amused when the dress dropped to her ankles.

Christian with his plastic pig on the stairs at Sophistocat

3
INDOORS
AND
OUTDOORS

Christian was always very calm and well behaved when he was in the flat above Sophistocat. Instead of racing around and chewing anything that took his fancy, he was content to wander from room to room investigating open cupboards and drawers, and occasionally having a drink in the bathroom.

Admittedly, before coming up to the flat he had usually been to his garden for a game of football, or it was at the end of the day, when he was content just to doze. In the wild, lions can sleep up to twenty hours a day, making them either the laziest of beasts or the most efficient conservers of energy.

Christian relaxes in the flat above Sophistocat

Christian with John and Ace on the stairs in the flat

Christian in the entrance hall of the flat

When Christian was taken to visit friends – and he did receive lots of invitations – we were always careful to consider potential dangers. Would he be safe from traffic? From other animals? How many people would be there? And, most importantly, did we think Christian would be happy? We knew he enjoyed going for drives in the car or in the Sophistocat van, so there was never any difficulty in loading him into the back seat. And we always kept him on his lead when walking him from the shop to the car, even though it was only a few paces.

On one of these outings we took Christian to a huge flat in Kensington, shared by three glamorous Australian girls we had known at university in Sydney. The trio had met Christian in the shop so we didn't anticipate any problems, and as we settled down to

Christian makes himself at home in the bathroom

a cup of coffee we allowed him to wander around the flat. There was no exit other than the front door, so we were not concerned when he disappeared down the hallway. Unfortunately, one of the girls was still in the bath and hadn't closed the door properly. Christian just nosed in and decided to have a drink from the bath. The resulting shrieks sent him scurrying back up the hall to the sitting room, where he decided to settle down for the rest of the afternoon. Our friend has rather dined out on the story ever since.

Of course, there were other friends who were less keen to meet Christian. But he loved meeting new people and, just like any domestic cat, was invariably drawn to those who were most wary of him. 'Just sit here and ignore him,' we would say to such nervous individuals, reassuring them that he had never bitten anyone. 'Have a cup of coffee and

we'll put him on the other side of the room.' After some time, the person would relax. Unfortunately, Christian had not lost interest. He would quietly work his way around the room and, when that person was innocently chatting away, would suddenly jump up and put a paw on them. The resulting kerfuffle, with screams and spilt coffee, delighted him. This was a result!

Christian would play a similar game in the shop, stalking us through the table legs or hiding behind chests of drawers, and deliberately contriving a situation where it appeared that *we* were hiding from *him*. If we spotted him, he would feign a sudden loss of interest and wander off to find something else to sniff or chew. It was all highly entertaining. And though it may sound anthropomorphic to interpret his behaviour in this way, there is no doubt that Christian was having fun.

Christian demands attention

As Christian grew larger, exercise became a more pressing concern. But where could we take him? This problem was solved when the Reverend Williamson, vicar of the Fetter Lane congregation of the Moravian Church, agreed that Christian could come to play in the Church's grounds on the King's Road, a few hundred yards from Sophistocat. We had been introduced to the vicar by our friends Rod and Joan Thomas, who rented a studio there. Known as the Moravian Close, this secluded sanctuary made an ideal playground for Christian, with its high entrance gate and ancient brick walls.

Remarkably few local residents were aware of the Moravian Close, hidden just feet from the bustling King's Road; Roy Hazle and Sandy Lloyd from Harrods were amazed when we showed it to them. The site had an interesting history. The land had originally been part of St Thomas Moore's Thames-side estate but was confiscated by Henry VIII in 1535 when Moore fell from favour. Subsequent illustrious owners of the site had included the Marquis of Winchester; Sir Robert Cecil, the first Earl of Salisbury; and Sir Hans Sloane, who bequeathed his founding collection to the British Museum. When the Moravian missionaries first came to England in 1742, from what is today modern Saxony, their London place of worship had been in Fetter Lane, off Fleet Street. The Close, behind Lindsey House on the Chelsea Embankment, had been the congregation's graveyard and became known as 'God's Acre'. After the Fetter Lane church was bombed during World War II, a spare studio here was converted to a church to serve the Fetter Lane congregation.

The Moravian Close represented the final jigsaw piece in Christian's London life. Every day he was taken there for his exercise. It was a chance to run free, explore the garden and spring ambushes from behind the hedges. The Moravians bury their dead vertically, so the headstones are flush with the ground, leaving the graveyard as an open space. Initially Christian hugged the hedges around the edge, but soon he became confident enough to race around in the middle, chasing footballs and – if we allowed him – us. Friends would often come to join in. If Christian ever became too rough, we would just stand still and stop the game.

John and Ace relax with Christian on the lawn in the Moravian Close

Christian was surprisingly gentle with children

Christian plays football in the Moravian Close

Although it was generally safe for children to play with Christian, we were always particularly careful. On one occasion in Sophistocat he had met a mother casually wandering around the shop dangling her toddler on walking reins. Intrigued, Christian had jumped down from the stairs at the back – his favourite viewing spot – and gently prodded the child. The mother was most alarmed, even though Christian had not been aggressive, and she left the shop promising to return with her husband. When he subsequently arrived, he was so amused by the idea that his son and heir had been prodded by a lion that the family became regular visitors and friends.

Accounts do exist of lions singling out children from groups of adults and attacking them, but Christian showed no such inclination. When another friend asked whether her son could come and play with Christian in the Close we were happy to agree. Christian just patted young Martin Fowler and stared at him curiously, then went off to chase his football. Blocks of flats overlook the Moravian Close and the residents would watch from their balconies and call down encouragement, waving and cheering, as Christian raced around. We never once received a complaint.

These play sessions gave us the first indication of just how lazy lions can be. After only half an hour

Christian chases after the football in the Moravian Close

or so in the Close, Christian was ready to go back to Sophistocat, particularly if it was raining. The occasional snow fall intrigued him, with much sniffing and tasting, but on those occasions the play sessions were particularly brief. The only real struggle with Christian was when we had to rub off all the mud before allowing him loose around the shop.

The Reverend Williamson was amused by Christian's visits, although he was a little dubious when Christian jumped up onto the roof of his car and resolutely refused to be budged. I was later to realise that this was typical lion behaviour: Christian's innate wish was to have an overview of his territory, just as George and Joy Adamson's lioness Elsa had often climbed onto their Land Rover.

Christian peers out between the coats of arms of the historic owners of the Moravian Close

4
LIFE ON THE KING'S ROAD

After Christian's arrival at Sophistocat, it did not take long for word to spread that there was a lion living in the shop and people frequently came in just to see him. But, as in Harrods, he was not always somewhere visible. In the wild, lions sleep during the day, frequently hunting by night when their night vision gives them an advantage over the game. At Sophistocat we reversed this natural cycle and Christian slept at night, often having to be woken in the mornings.

Driving down the King's Road in the Mercedes

Walks down the King's Road were not a success, even to the Moravian Close just a few hundred yards up the road. Christian accepted his lead for the few steps from the shop to the car. Any longer, however, and he would pull and tug, or simply sit down and wait to be carried. Even for a potentially short stroll to the nearby Casserole Restaurant – opposite Paulton Square, owned by friends Keith Lichtenstein and Dicky Kriese – it would thus always have to be a drive in the car. We would arrive towards the end of lunchtime, when just a few regulars lingered and the staff didn't have to worry about tripping over Christian. While we ate, he was happy to sit under the table and chew a bone the chef had put aside, particularly when the beautiful model Emma Breeze was happy to share her lunch with him.

Carrying Christian down the King's Road

Christian enjoys the ride in
the back of the Mercedes

The racing driver James Hunt was an old friend of Jennifer-Mary's, so on a visit to James' garage we decided to turn a social occasion into a photo shoot. James was very keen, and although he was then only at the beginning of his career, racing in Formula Three, we all agreed that the caption should be 'The

King of the Road meets the King of the Jungle'. An optimistic idea at the time, perhaps, but one that would prove accurate when in 1976 James beat his friend Niki Lauda to gain the coveted title of Formula One World Champion. By then Christian was already King of the Jungle, having been successfully rehabilitated in

48

James Hunt watches Christian clamber all over his fragile racing car

The King of the Jungle meets the King of the Road, James Hunt

Kenya. The photo shoot was pretty chaotic, but James was remarkably calm, despite Christian jumping onto his valuable but rather fragile car.

We also received many requests from people who wanted to hire Christian for events: parties, film premieres, promotions and so on. But our few experiences with Christian in public quickly curtailed any thought of accepting such invitations, even though the hefty fees would have helped us meet the feeding bills. Christian was just not comfortable in strange surroundings.

One commercial offer we did accept, however, was for a *Vanity Fair* magazine photo shoot. This featured lingerie from Barbara Hulaniki, who had created the Biba label and opened her iconic store on Kensington High Street, and Janet Reger: two very clever ladies who were carving out successful careers. Our stipulation, however, was that the photo shoot had to be at Sophistocat rather than in Biba or in a photo studio. In the spirit of *Vanity Fair's* glamour image, Marc Tracy at Tod's hairdressers opposite Sophistocat gave Christian a brush and blow dry!

Christian with a British Airways stewardess – looking for an upgrade?

Marc Tracy giving Christian a brush and blow-dry before his *Vanity Fair* photoshoot.

Christian with model for *Vanity Fair's* 'Nights on the Wild Side' photoshoot

Christian was totally unfazed by this frivolity at Tod's and the other customers who were accustomed to seeing rock stars being pampered were greatly amused. So, ready for his close-up, Christian posed on a bed with the model for the *Nights on the Wild Side* photo series. The model's flowing blonde hair intrigued Christian, who always liked testing things for their taste and texture. Eventually the photographer got the required shots, but there was rather a lot of wasted time because Christian was intent on trying to chew the model's hair, despite her plaintive objections that her face was her fortune.

A much easier shoot was created by Derek, who had been asked by one of the Fleet Street tabloids to come up with some ideas for an Easter theme photo series. He rang me to suggest he bring some baby chicks to Sophistocat and photograph them with Christian. Although I was rather skeptical, the resulting photos were just what the paper wanted.

Amazingly, all the chicks survived.

It was an invitation to appear on the popular *Blue Peter* children's television programme that brought an end to Christian's career as a model. During a pre-filming rehearsal in the studio Christian behaved impeccably and was intrigued by all the activity with cameras and crew, but by the time the live appearance was to be filmed, he had become bored. Instead of a calm chat on the sofa with the delightful Valerie Singleton, it was a wrestling match to try and keep Christian from running off.

Ace and I decided that such events were too stressful for Christian. Still, he had at least earned £90 for his appearances, and Jennifer-Mary took him to our bank manager Mr Nash, at the Nat West branch in the King's Road, to open his own account. This sum paid for only three week's feed bills, but we all agreed that Christian had done more than enough modelling.

Christian fascinated by a clutch of day-old chicks in an Easter-themed photoshoot

Christian having lunch with model Emma Breeze and friends at the Casserole restaurant on the King's Road

One final public appearance, however, was as a favour to the popular radio presenter Jack de Manio, who asked whether Christian would come on his early morning BBC Breakfast programme. Jack was our neighbour, so of course we agreed and set off early one morning to the BBC headquarters in Portland Place.

'No dogs are allowed in the BBC,' said the uniformed Commissionaire, when we arrived. 'What about lions?' we countered, and swept inside before he could find an answer. Unfortunately, despite vigorous encouragement from us and Jack, Christian refused to roar. In fact, by this stage he had never mustered more than a few grunts. Jack was a true professional and managed to keep his listeners amused but the *Daily Mail* was less impressed. The following day saw a large photo of Christian across a double-page spread under a banner headline that read: 'Mike-shy Christian flops on Radio.'

Jennifer-Mary Taylor takes Christian to the National Westminster Bank to open his bank account

Ace and Jennifer-Mary lead Christian into the studios of the BBC

Christian meets popular BBC radio presenter Jack de M

All this was great fun, but the plain truth was that Christian was not comfortable away from Sophistocat or the Moravian Close. He was also growing rapidly and would soon be too big for his home at the shop.

At this point, we began considering Longleat Safari Park on the Marquis of Bath's estate in Somerset as Christian's future home. After all, this was where some of the lions used in *Born Free* had been relocated after the filming had been completed.

Longleat Safari Park had been established in 1966 as a partnership between Jimmy Chipperfield of Chipperfield's Circus and the Seventh Marquis of Bath. Faced with death duties, high taxes and the huge costs of maintaining one of Britain's great ancestral houses, the Marquis was one of the first stately home owners to go commercial and open his home to the public. Longleat Safari Park was the first drive-through safari park outside Africa, and although we knew that there had been problems at the beginning, with the introduction of lions from different prides, and concerns from neighbouring farmers, by 1970 these had been resolved and it was a popular success.

So perhaps Longleat was the answer. But would they be prepared to incorporate Christian into one of the existing prides or would they capitalise on his amenable character and use him in advertisements and films? The safari park was basically a commercial operation, with high overheads, and although we respected the managers, Mary Chipperfield and her husband Roger Cawley, for their knowledge and love of lions, we were concerned that Christian might not find himself living 'free' in the actual park.

While pondering this dilemma, with Jennifer-Mary, John, Joe, Unity, Kay and Derek – Christian's human pride, a totally unexpected alternative arose. The actors Bill Travers and his wife Virginia McKenna, who had played the roles of George and Joy Adamson in the film *Born Free*, were in London to visit Virginia's dress-maker, a neighbour of ours in the World's End. He must have told them that there was a lion living

Christian hides under a table at Sophistocat

nearby, so while Virginia was planning her movie star wardrobe, Bill wandered over to Sophistocat to investigate – while ostensibly looking for a pine desk.

At that stage, none of us had seen *Born Free*, but fortunately Jennifer-Mary recognised Bill, and so we introduced him to Christian. Because of their experience with lions during the filming, Bill and Virginia knew far more about them than we did and they immediately acknowledged that Christian was an exceptional individual. They subsequently explained that *Born Free* had been a tough experience, with both of them attacked and injured during the filming. Only once we had seen the film,

which showed no suggestion of such dangers, did we realise what an incredible acting job they had done.

Bill and Ginny wanted to know where we planned to take Christian when he outgrew Sophistocat – and London. We admitted that we were still trying to find the best solution. They put their heads together and a few days later Bill rang with an idea. He had contacted George Adamson in Kenya to ask whether he would consider the challenge of rehabilitating Christian there.

Now that was a challenge for us, too. It called for an immediate conference of Christian's human pride. Take Christian back to Africa? A fifth-generation zoo-bred lion? Would he survive?

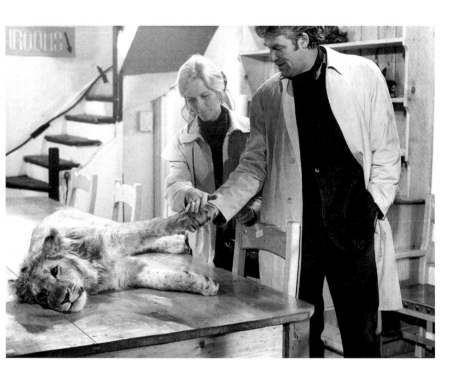

Christian's first meeting at Sophistocat with actors Bill Travers and Virginia McKenna, stars of *Born Free*

5
PREPARING FOR AFRICA

Once the decision had been made to fly Christian to Kenya and place him in the care of George Adamson, we had to wait for the Kenyan government to grant their approval. They were accustomed to approving the export of lions from Kenya, so there was some initial confusion when an application arrived to *import* one!

Meanwhile, Christian was rapidly outgrowing Sophistocat so Bill and Ginny kindly offered us temporary accommodation at Gamekeeper's Cottage, their home near Dorking. Here they had a large garden with enough space to build a temporary enclosure, in which a colourful gypsy caravan had been installed for Christian to sleep in.

Christian playing with Derek at Gamekeeper's Cottage in Dorking, home of Bill Travers and Virginia McKenna

Christian's life in Dorking (clockwise from top left): an introduction to Virginia's dogs; relaxing in the caravan; meeting young Will Travers, Bill and Virginia's son

Christian with John and Ace in Dorking

Before leaving London, we filmed a re-staging of the meeting between Bill, Virginia and Christian in Sophistocat, and of Christian playing football in the Moravian Close. For the latter, director James Hill, who directed *The Bellstone Fox*, also with Bill Travers, shot footage in slow motion. The noise from the high-speed camera distracted Christian and every time filming began he would stop and stare at it, spoiling the footage. 'Is there anything you can do to keep him playing football?' asked James. There was. We allowed Christian to chase us instead of the ball, thus negating months of patient 'training'. Christian couldn't believe his luck: this was the opportunity he had long been waiting for, and he totally ignored the camera as he chased us around the garden.

George Adamson was later fascinated by this footage: he had never before had the opportunity of watching a lion running in slow motion, and was able to admire Christian's powerful chest, rippling muscles, taut sinews and sheer power. Derek had also been on hand to photograph the antics, and the shot he took of Christian gleefully tackling me won the 1970 Ilford World Press Award for Best Feature Picture.

Many friends visited us in Dorking while we were waiting to leave for Kenya. Early one morning we even had an outing to West Wittering, on the Sussex coast, to show Christian the sea – just as George and Joy had once taken Elsa to the Indian Ocean at Kiunga on one of their safaris. Christian was not impressed by the beach, however, and Ace and I had to sprint up the sand to catch him as he raced away from the waves. We did wonder what later visitors would make of the distinctive lion pad marks.

Christian tackles John during a game of football in the Moravian Close, an image that won Derek the 1970 Ilford World Press Award for Best Feature Picture

Virginia, Ace, Bill and John with
Christian at West Wittering
Beach, West Sussex

ABOVE: Unity Bevis playing wheelbarrows with Christian

OPPOSITE: John feeding Christian his favourite
bone marrow

On 12 August 1970 Christian celebrated his first, and last, birthday in England. Unity came down from London with a special mincemeat cake, and we gave him a huge marrow bone.

Running Sophistocat and looking after Christian had so far left little time for background reading. But now, while we waited for the Kenyan government to grant permission for Christian to be flown out, I was able to read *Born Free*, Joy Adamson's account of life with her lion Elsa, published in 1960, and her husband George's biography *Bwana Game*, published in 1968.

These books were to be the start of my now substantial library of Africana. They not only taught me about lions but were my introduction to the colonial history of East Africa, with its early settlers and the ranching projects, like those of the third Lord Delamare and Gilbert Colville, in which British farmers had to experiment with cross-breeding European stock with local breeds to try and combat local diseases.

There was fascinating reading about the great hunting expeditions, when Kenya teemed with game and such celebrated 'white hunters' as Denys Finch Hatton, Eric Rundgren and Baron Bror Fredrik von Blixen-Finecke brought back tales of daring. I also learned about the extravagant lives of the Happy Valley residents, including such scandals as the murder of Lord Erroll, and caught up on Kenya's more recent history, from the Mau Mau insurgence to the first independent government under President Jomo Kenyatta.

Joy Adamson and Elsa in Meru National Park ELSA TRUST

George Adamson with Elsa on Elsa's rock, Meru National Park ELSA TRUST

Of particular interest and relevance, though, was the history of the Kenya Game Department and its challenge of monitoring the wildlife. George Adamson had been a game warden based in the Northern Frontier Department (NFD) when he had been forced to shoot Elsa's mother in 1956. He and his friend Ken Smith had been asked by local farmers to kill a lioness that had been taking their cattle – it was a game warden's job to remove stock-killing lions and other destructive wildlife – but it

Joy Adamson and Elsa in Meru ELSA TRUST

was only after shooting Elsa's mother that George realised she was lactating. When George found the three young cubs concealed in a rocky crevice he decided to bring them back to his wife Joy at their house in Isiolo.

Born Friederike Victoria Gessner in Silesia, Austro-Hungary (now Opava, Czech Republic), Joy had come to Kenya in 1937 and married George Adamson, her third husband, in 1944. She had recently completed a government commission of

Elsa asleep in George's tent
and on his camp bed, Meru
ELSA TRUST

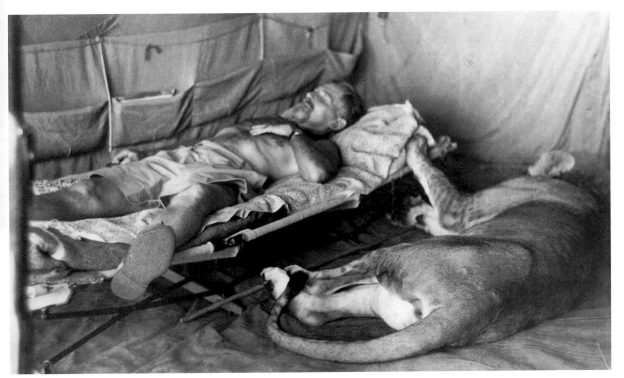

75

over five hundred detailed paintings of tribesmen in their traditional dress. (Today these paintings are stored in the vaults of the Nairobi museum, but Joy's book *Peoples of Kenya* reveals her skill and dedication and remains an important historic record of Kenya's colourful cultural diversity.) Unable to have children, Joy had long since transferred her maternal instincts to a continuous stream of different of animals. George knew that with time on her hands after completing the commission, she would be happy to foster the cubs.

Other people had raised lions from cubs: in Zambia's Luangwa Valley, for example, British conservationist Norman Carr had raised two males. But most had ended up in zoos. Joy didn't want that happening to these cubs. When the game department insisted that she surrender them, she and George compromised: they agreed reluctantly that two should go to Rotterdam Zoo at Blijdorp in the Netherlands, while the smallest, which they named Elsa, stayed with them. The story of George and Joy's successfully raising and rehabilitation of Elsa is immortalised in Joy's book *Born Free* and the subsequent film of the same name. Sadly, Elsa was only four years old when she died of tick fever, but by then she had produced three cubs, which George later released in the Serengeti.

Rehabilitating Elsa was a difficult process, particularly as she was alone. Lions hunt most effectively as a team and George always regretted agreeing that Elsa's sisters be taken from him.

Perhaps this was why Elsa remained very much a 'lioness of two worlds', as a young David Attenborough so perceptively described her. During Elsa's time with George and Joy she would habitually wander off by herself to hunt and mate but then return to visit. The most dramatic return was when she bought her three cubs across the Uaso Nyiro river to the Adamsons' camp in Meru and introduced them.

Attenborough made a number of interesting observations while working on his documentary about Joy and George. He had not been prepared for his first meeting with Elsa, who woke him from a nap by jumping on top of him, alarming him not only with her weight but also her 'appalling halitosis'. He saw how Joy was totally besotted with her lion, and even ordered George to shoot a wild lion that was threatening 'my Elsa' – a demand that George ignored. But it was this very passion that made *Born Free* a worldwide best seller. Elsa was a unique lioness, just as Christian had his own unique personality, and Joy managed to convey this through her stories. It was only later, when surprised by George's lack of personal funds, that I discovered how Joy had kept all the royalties, arguing that George had 'only written a few pages'.

The story of Elsa confirmed to me that we had made the right decision to entrust Christian's future to George. What adventures Christian would have! What's more, we would be lucky enough to share his first weeks in Africa with him.

George Adamson with Elsa, Meru ELSA TRUST

6
OUT TO AFRICA

Finally, we were to leave England. The waiting had been frustrating, both for us and for Christian. Dorking had felt claustrophobic after our free-wheeling life on the King's Road, and for Bill Travers and Virginia McKenna, who led a cosy family life at Gamekeeper's Cottage, the comings and goings of our London friends at odd hours must have been disruptive. But we all muddled along until it was time to leave.

John, Christian and Ace at Kampi ya Simba, 'The camp of lions', Kora

The important thing was that Christian was safe and healthy. The only glitch came when, in an unexpected display of alpha male dominance, he once grabbed Bill with uncharacteristic aggression. No real harm was done, but it was a disappointment to me and Ace that Christian and Bill never really bonded. There was nothing we could do to change Christian's attitude.

At Dorking, Christian was becoming accustomed to his crate, which we had designed with horizontal bars, rather than the normal vertical ones. We had reasoned that if Christian pawed the bars he would be less likely to damage his paws this way. Flatteringly, the crate manufacturers were so impressed that they subsequently altered the construction of their travelling crates for all exotic animals. We played with Christian in and around the crate, fed him in it, and locked him in for longer and longer periods so that when we closed the door for the final time he was not too distressed.

When George Adamson finally secured the official approval for Christian to fly to Kenya we all celebrated. Christian's rehabilitation in Kenya was fast becoming a reality. At last we were off. At Heathrow, we were driven straight onto the tarmac and directly to the loading bay of the Kenya Airways Boeing 727. Asked by the airline to weigh Christian, we 'guestimated' a fairly haphazard figure of about 175 pounds. Nobody at Heathrow seemed prepared to dispute it.

We also received a request that the film company making the documentary about Christian's rehabilitation should insure Heathrow for a million pounds while Christian was being transported. The idea that this little cub, who had cost just 250 guineas less than a year ago, might cause this amount of damage at an international airport seemed pretty far-fetched. Thankfully there were no hitches, and Christian was loaded safely onto the 'plane. Virginia McKenna came to see us off and shed a few poignant

Christian lying on his crate, Dorking

Weighing Christian in preparation for his flight to Nairobi; he tipped the scales at
175 pounds

tears – perhaps from relief! Christian and his owners would no longer be living in her garden and her dogs had all survived.

On 23rd August 1970 Christian touched down on African soil. His ancestral homeland. The flight had included a stopover in Paris, where we checked on him and were relieved to find him calm and sleepy. At Nairobi's Jomo Kenyatta Airport, however, he was agitated and called to us continually as he moved around his crate. For the first time in his life he no longer smelled musky, fresh and clean, but was stale and dry, perhaps from sweating in the heat and discomfort of the plane. Even his eyes were bleary – but then so were mine, having been awake throughout the long overnight flight wondering whether Christian was safe in the hold below.

Unloading Christian was a prolonged and frustrating process. Security and protocol for 'livestock' meant that Christian's crate had to be cleared by customs and immigration before he could be released into a secure holding area. It was immediately apparent that none of these officials were anxious to inspect Christian too closely. Indeed, from the attention

Checking Christian's crate at Heathrow Airport, with help from Bill Travers and Virginia McKenna

George Adamson meets Christian for the first time, with John, Ace and Bill Travers
at Nairobi Airport

he attracted, it was clear that many had never seen a lion before – or certainly not one as tame as Christian.

George Adamson was there to meet us, anxious to make Christian's acquaintance and to oversee his unloading and transfer from the aircraft. We were apprehensive: at last we were to meet the great lion guru: the man who had rehabilitated the famous Elsa, and in whose hands Christian's destiny now lay. He was a much slighter figure than I had expected and almost dapper, in his neat goatee beard and pressed safari suit. I later appreciated that this was for the benefit of the film company and the special occasion of Christian's arrival.

Adamson carefully studied us with his clear blue eyes, but his real focus was on Christian. He was impressed by his size and condition and, flatteringly, by his affection for Ace and me. Commenting on Christian's lush coat and burgeoning new mane, he explained that no one-year-old wild lion from Kenya would be as impressive as Christian.

In subsequent correspondence, George explained how the challenge of rehabilitating a fifth-generation lion from England fascinated him, but admitted that he had some initial misgivings about Christian's owners.

The idea had appealed to me greatly, not only because it would save Christian from a lifetime of captivity but also because it would be, in all probability, the first time an English-born lion had been returned to the life for which he was created. I felt confident that his inherited knowledge and instincts would soon assert themselves, given the chance, and in spite of his breeding.

I must admit that I did not feel the same confidence about his two owners, when I heard that they would accompany Christian and stay for a few weeks in my camp. I had been led to believe they were very 'mod', with long hair and exotic clothing. My first sight at Nairobi Airport of pink bell-bottom trousers and flowing locks did nothing to dispel my misgivings. But Ace and John soon restored my faith in the modern generation. Immediately, I sensed the bond of deep affection and trust between them and Christian. I know from experience how hard it must have been for them to leave Christian to face the inevitable dangers and hardships of a lion in the wild.

Kora, 15th July 1971

Christian in the back of George's Landrover on the journey to Kora

After two days in the airport holding compound, where Christian had become a huge attraction, it was time to set off for Kora, two hundred and fifty miles to the north. When George backed his Land Rover into the compound, Christian was happy to jump into the back. He had always loved driving around in cars in London and had become bored by the cement enclosure at the airport. He must have been surprised to find straw to lie on, rather than the leather of a Mercedes or Bentley, and bemused by the wire mesh panel between the front seats and the rear of the car – George's standard fitting, used for transporting lions that were unhabituated so far less friendly. But he was unfazed; happy to stand and look out the back, from where he attracted considerable attention whenever we slowed in local traffic or refuelled.

George had decided that the journey should be broken into two stages and had commissioned his old friend Nevil Baxendale to build a temporary camp halfway to Kora, with a small enclosure for Christian. The drive to Nevil's camp was long and hot, and Christian lay panting in the back of the car while Ace and I took turns travelling up front with George, both eager to further gauge his reaction to Christian.

During the final stretch, as we travelled through increasingly inhospitable country, I realised that Christian needed a loo break. I rather tentatively asked George – or Mr Adamson, as I was still calling him at this stage – to stop. George was sceptical. 'If he runs off here, we'll never catch him,' he said. I insisted that Christian wasn't going anywhere, and opened the rear of the Land Rover. Christian looked around gingerly. It was hot, and when he jumped down he found the road dry and rocky, a far cry from the soft green grass of the Moravian Close. He sniffed the unfamiliar air, did his business and then, as soon as I encouraged him, jumped straight back into the Land Rover. George had watched all this while quietly sucking on his pipe. 'That was quite

remarkable. He is a fine young lion,' he said, as I closed the door behind him and got back into the passenger seat. 'Please call me George.'

Bravo Christian! I beamed with pride and couldn't wait to tell Ace.

When we arrived at Nevil's camp we took Christian for his first proper walk in Africa. This casual stroll soon took on a more significant dimension when Christian spotted something in the bush and immediately crouched and froze. It was a lost *gombi* (the local name for a cow). We watched in fascination as Christian stalked his prey, creeping slowly forward and using the low bushes

Christian meets the nervous camp staff upon his arrival at Kora

Temporary camp on the banks of the Tana River, Kora

to conceal himself. George was worried: though only a domestic cow, this beast had substantial horns and could prove dangerous to an inexperienced young lion. He ran to get his Land Rover and drive it between the two animals. Undeterred, Christian dodged the vehicle – forcing us, in desperation, to grab him. For the first time ever, he snarled at us, making very clear that he was not happy we'd frustrated his efforts.

Although we were rather shaken by this warning, George was impressed by Christian's instinctive stalking. It convinced him that rehabilitating Christian should prove no more difficult than it had been with African-born lions. That night in camp Christian was wonderfully affectionate. Perhaps it was the excitement of this first stalking, or perhaps he was trying to make up for his earlier aggression. Either way, however, he was not impressed by having to sleep on the ground, and eventually dozed off with a pillow and a paw on my face for reassurance. London's comforts were not too distant a memory, even amidst all this excitement. Just Like Elsa before him, Christian eventually took over a camp bed for himself.

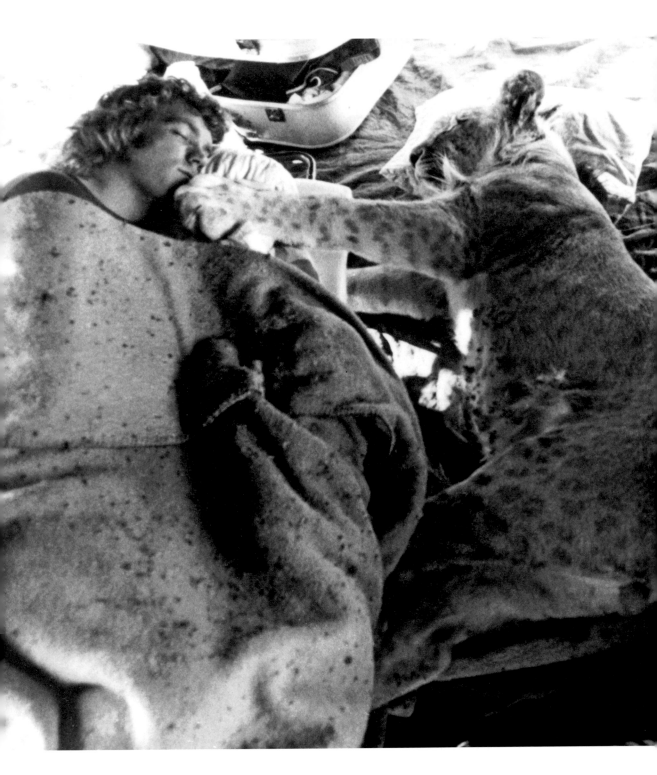

Christian and John get some rest on the first night in camp

Christian claims the camp bed at Kora

Derek takes a light meter reading from Christian JOHN RENDALL

As we approached Kora the next day, George suggested we walk the last few miles, so that Christian could start learning the smells and noises of his new home. This entrance track had been cleared by George's brother Terence, who had spent his life building roads, bridges and accommodation all over Kenya. Born in India, where their father had been in colonial service, the two boys had been educated at Dean Close School in Cheltenham, but both had subsequently settled in Kenya to pursue a life in the bush that they both loved and knew so well.

In 1968, Terence had retired to his modest home in Malindi. His last job had been at Galana, which was the largest cattle ranch in Kenya and funded by a wealthy American, Martin Anderson, in partnership with two Kenyan visionaries, Mike Prettejohn and Gilfrid Powys. This dynamic trio had dreamed of combining commercial cattle ranching with safaris and indigenous wildlife. With the initial support of Jomo Kenyatta, Kenya's founding president, Galana was eventually to run over 26,000 head of cattle. In 1968 however, this ambitious project was still in its infancy.

Terence Adamson, George's brother, building the new camp at Kora with one of his team

John and Christian walking through the bush at Kora

It was Terence whose engineering skills were required to survey and build new roads, and to clear the only airstrip, last used by legendary white hunter and lover of Karen Blixen, Denys Finch Hatton in the 1930s.

For George's new camp, Terence was summoned from his retirement with the challenge of clearing a track to Kora and building a camp there. He happily accepted when he heard that there were elephants, his favourite animal, in the area. When we arrived at the Tana River, Terence had already got the temporary camp up, while Kampi Ya Simba (the Camp of Lions) was being completed a few miles inland.

We spent the first few days walking and exploring the banks of the Tana with Christian. This river dominates the Kora area and is the Piccadilly Circus gathering place for all the local wildlife, particularly in the early evening. Walking with Christian was exhilarating. With his collar and lead abandoned, he could now run free to investigate every new sight, sound and smell. From the riverbank he could watch hippos surfacing and blowing in irritation at our intrusion, and observe the baboons and vervet monkeys that barked and shrieked their warnings.

George encouraged these walks, both to toughen up Christian's pads and help him acclimatise to the heat. In only a few days Christian would be meeting the first lions he had seen since he had been separated from his sister at Harrods over a year ago. When George left for Naivasha to collect Boy and Katania, we enjoyed our last few precious days alone with him.

Christian leaps between rocks in the Tana River to avoid getting his paws wet

Christian at sunset on the Tana River with Ace and John

John, Ace and Christian beside the Tana River

Christian drinking from the Tana River

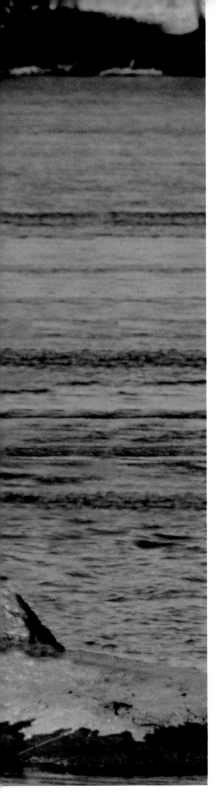

Christian with Ace and John on the
banks of the Tana River

Ace and John with Christian in camp, Kora

7

JOINING
THE PRIDE

Terence had now completed the lion enclosures at Kora Rock, some three miles inland from the Tana. Known as Kampi Ya Simba, the 'Camp of lions', this would become George's permanent campsite. The landscape here was in dramatic contrast to the comparative lushness of the Tana riverbanks: in place of graceful doum palms and lush riverine greenery were thorny acacias and dense *Commiphora* bush. The camp's position high above the river provided welcome breezes and panoramic views. All was ready for the arrival of Boy and Katania. But were we and Christian?

Boy pauses to mark his territory on a walk with Christian and George

The history of George's other lions was a complex one. After the filming of *Born Free,* the film company had disposed of every piece of scenery and property used during the filming. George and Joy had been shocked to realise that this 'garage sale' included the lions. They could not comprehend how the film company Columbia, or the producer Carl Foreman, having been so enthusiastic about telling the story of Elsa's return to the wild, could then sell the lion 'actors' back into captivity. Especially not when they had on hand George Adamson, world expert on lions and a pivotal character in the film, who was willing and able to rehabilitate them.

Despite the pleas from George and Joy, Bill Travers and Virginia McKenna, Columbia stood firm. The lions were to be sold: to Detroit Zoo in America, and to Paignton Zoo and Whipsnade in England. Seven also went to Longleat in Wiltshire, the very place where we had once considered sending Christian and certainly the best of the unhappy options.

But there were three lions that they had been unable to sell: Ugas, who had come from the orphanage at Nairobi National Park; and Boy and Girl, who had been the regimental mascots of the Second Battalion of the Scots Guards based in Kenya. The latter two had been hand-reared by Colour Sergeant Ryves, together with his wife Hildegarde and their daughters Patricia and Jenny. When the regiment returned to the UK, the cubs had remained in Kenya – the suggestion that the regiment keep them as mascots in the UK was rejected, nobody being comfortable with the idea of lions on parade outside Buckingham Palace – and George was delighted when Sergeant Ryves and his regimental sergeant, Major Campbell Graham, gave him permission to rehabilitate them. George also acquired four other lions, Sally, Shaitana, Suki and Suswa, which had been lent to the film company by the Marchese Suki Bisletti, a glamorous Kenyan resident.

George was delighted with this opportunity but urgently needed to find an area in which to release his new charges. Good news came when Ted Goss, an old friend of George's and now Warden of Meru National Park, granted him permission to bring Boy and Girl, and later Ugas and the Bisletti lions, to Meru. Joy had been extremely generous to Meru County Council and the Meru Reserve from the proceeds of *Born Free*, so George and his lions were welcome there. George was assisted in the rehabilitations by his god-son Johnny Baxendale, son of his old friend Nevil Baxendale, with whom he had enjoyed many adventures over the years, including a failed gold prospecting expedition and a crossing of Lake Rudolph in 1934 in a boat improvised from hide and acacia branches.

At first all went well with the rehabilitations. But one day, while driving through the park, Johnny met up with Boy who jumped onto his Land Rover and refused to move. While Johnny waited for Boy to get bored, the new warden Peter Jenkins (who had replaced Ted Goss) drove up with his family. As Johnny and Peter chatted, Boy jumped down, pushed his head into Peter's car and grabbed Peter's young son Mark.

Fortunately, Peter was able to start the car and speed away, throwing Boy to the ground. Mark sustained a scratch on his head and a deep bite to his arm, however, and the incident led to calls for George to shoot Boy. Only because of the concerns of the Director of National Parks, that the shooting of one of the *Born Free* lions would attract negative publicity for Kenya, was Boy spared. As a condition, George and Joy were required to leave Meru and abandon their rehabilitation programmes. Indeed, Peter Jenkins gave George two options: shoot Boy or remove him from the Park.

Before they could leave Meru, however, Joy discovered Boy in a serious condition: badly wounded, with a broken right foreleg, and seriously

Boy is king of his new domain at Kora

Boy snarls, revealing the patches on his forehead rubbed bare by the bars of his travelling crate

emaciated. Sticking through his cheek were the quills of a porcupine – probably all that the wounded lion had been able to catch. George contacted the husband and wife veterinarians Tony and Sue Haarthorn, who immediately flew to Meru to assess Boy's chances of recovery. No one was better qualified than this pair, who had worked on Operation Noah, the evacuation of over 6,000 animals after the building of the Kariba Dam on the Zambezi river in the late 1950s. Their experience was to prove invaluable to George over the years and on this occasion it enabled them to save Boy.

At a makeshift operating theatre built by George, Tony and Sue inserted two metal pins into the lion's shattered foreleg. This incredibly complicated operation proved a success.

Boy began his recovery at Elsamere, Joy Adamson's home on Lake Naivasha. George did not want to keep him here, where life was too claustrophobic for them both, and he knew that he could not take him back to Meru. To release a mature male lion elsewhere would not be easy, however, particularly as he had not fully recovered. Boy would need help, both from George and from other lions.

Boy asleep on his crate after arriving at Kora

Ideally, he would have his own pride, with a younger habituated lion to offer support. Serendipitously, it was at this point that George first heard about Christian in London.

In April 1970, I received a letter from my friend Bill Travers, telling me about Christian, a fifth-generation English lion, and asking whether I would be prepared to take him over and rehabilitate him back into the wild of his forebears. The idea appealed to me greatly, not only because it would save Christian from a life-time in captivity, but because it would be, in all probability, the first time an English lion had been returned to the life for which he had been created.

Letter from George Adamson

Enthused by the opportunity and challenge of rehabilitating Christian, George began looking for somewhere to release Boy and Christian. It would have to be a remote area, away from people and livestock, and an area without too many resident lions who, naturally, would defend their territory against these newcomers. George eventually focused on the Garissa area and, finally, the Kora Game Reserve, where there were few people or cattle. Fortunately, George's old friend Ken Smith, who had been with him when he shot Elsa's mother, had been promoted from Provincial Game Warden in the Garissa area to the Ministry of Wildlife and Tourism, and was able immediately to approve George's application. The Tana River Council were also in favour of the scheme, as George had agreed to pay an annual rent of £750 to the reserve and they hoped that he would provide some employment for local people.

George with Boy and Katania

Boy's relationship with Katania was an unusual example of a friendship between a mature male lion and an unrelated cub

John meets Boy at Kora

While George was finalising these negotiations he was offered an orphaned two-month-old female cub. He was thrilled by this stroke of luck as his prospective new pride – comprising just two males, Boy and Christian – was looking distinctly one-sided. He named the cub Katania and was surprised when Boy instantly accepted her. It is unusual for an adult male to be so receptive to young cubs and George assumed that Boy was simply missing the company of fellow lions.

The journey from Elsamere was long and arduous. When George arrived back at camp with Boy and Katania, both were exhausted and Boy had rubbed a raw patch on his forehead, adding to his rather sinister appearance. The two new lions were unloaded into the large compound which adjoined Christian's – where, for reassurance in his unfamiliar new home, we had left the crate in which he had been flown from England.

Christian was fascinated by the new arrivals. He crept around from behind his crate to investigate but Boy immediately charged the wire to chase him away. This went on for the next two days: every time Christian approached, Boy charged and Christian cowered in submission. Katania, who had been watching from a distance, eventually decided to creep towards Christian to greet him through the wire. She became the go-between, while Boy watched jealously.

We, too, had to meet Boy. One night he slept in our tent and took my arm in his jaws. It was very obvious as this huge lion stared into my face that he was asserting his position as alpha male of the pride. I wasn't about to contest this, and my voice had risen several octaves as I called out to George for help. To complicate matters Katania had also decided to sleep in our tent and was proceeding to chew my toes.

Katania reaching up to greet Christian

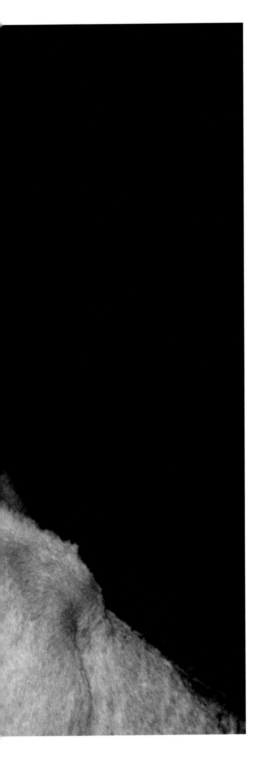

George reassured us that this was all part of normal lion behaviour: the animals had to introduce themselves and make the hierarchy clear.

George decided to take advantage of the interest Katania had shown in Christian and use her as an ambassador between the two males. He made a small hatch between the two compounds, allowing Katania to come and meet Christian. When she did so, Christian was thrilled and leapt forward to play with her. Katania was unfazed: she had done an exceptional thing by winning Boy over so a mere stripling like Christian was not going to intimidate her. She snarled at him and made it quite clear she was not afraid. Christian was bemused but undeterred, and followed her around; he was fascinated by the first lion he had met since he left Harrods. Boy grimaced at Christian's smell when Katania returned to his compound, but George assured us this was progress.

George helps Katania through the fence between her enclosure and Christian's

George with Christian and Katania

Katania's rapport with Christian allowed her to play an intermediary role between Christian and Boy

After a few days of Katania fraternising with Christian, George suggested that Boy and Christian should meet – but still keeping the chicken-wire fence between them. Up until this point, Christian had been sneaking closer to Boy, peeking from behind his crate. This more direct confrontation proved traumatic: Boy charged the wire, roaring his dominance and Christian cowered behind us, knocking me over and snarling at Ace. Christian had been taken from his parents when he was only a few days old so he would never have seen his father, Butch. The sight of a full-grown lion must have been extraordinary and intimidating.

Boy's roaring and charging went on for three more days – until eventually George decided that because Christian had correctly deferred to him, by crouching down and making the appropriate whimpering noises, it was time for the lions to meet in the open. He was confident that Boy would not kill Christian.

What could we say? We had to trust George, so the next day we led Christian out onto the rock behind Kampi ya Simba, where we knew Boy and Katania had settled for the day. Christian was alert and excited when he saw Boy and Katania. I sat beside him for reassurance. It seemed hours before

Christian observes Boy through the fence with a mixture of fear and curiosity

Boy charges at Christian, safe on his side of the fence

John introduces Christian to Boy for the first time outside their enclosures

Boy attacks Christian, who rolls over in instinctive submission

Derek walking with Christian at Kora JOHN RENDALL

anything happened: Boy feigned a lack of interest and Katania was content to keep close to him. But eventually Katania got bored and wandered over to greet Christian. That was too much for Boy and he suddenly stood up and charged.

Our hearts were in our mouths. Would Boy kill Christian? Would all our love and care be wiped out in an instant? Boy ran at Cristian and bowled him over. Christian howled with fear but again followed lion protocol by totally submitting to Boy and exposing his vulnerable belly. Satisfied, Boy retreated, and while he ostentiatiously ignored the shaken Christian, Katania came back to offer consolation. Ace and I held back: we dared not interfere in this lion drama. Thankfully, Christian had behaved correctly. Boy's position had been asserted, and it was with enormous relief that we could retire to camp.

Boy's demonstrations of dominance were repeated every day, but the charges gradually grew less ferocious until finally the three lions were able to lie together – although Boy would still give Christian a clout if he crept too close. The whole stressful process took about ten days. Once we saw that Christian was not going to be killed and that he was tentatively making his way in the lion world, George suggested we should leave camp for a while and see some of Kenya. He was right, of course, and though we felt unsure about leaving Christian so soon, we knew we had to make the break.

George's friend Monty Ruben had arranged a vehicle for us and we set off on safari to explore Christian's new country. My diary notes that the highlight of this safari was meeting Ian and Oria Douglas-Hamilton at their elephant camp at Lake Manyara, where their young daughter Saba (who many years later was to be a presenter of the *Big Cat Diary* television series) played safely with the elephants. We also went to the camp of American photographer Peter Beard in the Ngong Hills. Karen Blixen's cook, Kamante, was still working for Peter and happy to chat about his mistress and the eclectic guests whom she had entertained.

The other, rather more traumatic, episode on this trip took place when, while we were driving towards Nairobi, we spotted President Kenyatta's motor cavalcade racing towards us and waved in cheery greeting. The president's entourage did not appreciate our enthusiasm. They forced our Land Rover off the road and, ignoring our protests, beat us with the back of their pangas and slashed our tyres. Some years later when I met President Kenyatta at State House in Nairobi, I asked why his bodyguards had been so aggressive. He was most apologetic and explained that he had always had trouble curbing their enthusiasm.

After these adventures Ace and I returned to Kora to see how Christian was coping. The film crew, who had been making the documentary about his rehabilitation, had returned to England, so we were looking forward to a very special time with George and the lions without having to worry about cameras. But all was not well. Christian was sick – for the first time in his life. When we arrived, we found a listless young lion with alarmingly white gums. 'He has tick fever,' George told us. My diary records my shock: 'Christian sick? It can't be possible. That's what killed Elsa.' George injected Christian with Berenil and, thankfully, it had the desired result: within 24 hours he had recovered. If George had had this drug when Elsa was ill he believed he could have saved her.

Now it really was time to leave. Christian had been accepted by Boy, he had survived tick fever and he was now taking his first steps towards a successful rehabilitation. Our parting was emotional, but we knew Christian was safe with George, Boy and Katania. What more could we ask?

8
TRAGEDY AND REUNION

By January 1971 we were back in England. George was an excellent correspondent and wrote regularly with news of Christian and his adventures. We thus learned how Boy, Christian and Katania were now following George's routine of daily walks to familiarise them with their new territory and the other inhabitants of Kora Reserve.

George with Boy and Christian, searching the Tana River for the missing Katania

George walking with Boy and Christian Tony Fitzjohn (GAWPT)

George relaxing with Boy
and Christian on the banks
of the Tana River

For Boy, of course, the zebra, waterbuck, giraffe, baboon, elephant and rhino were familiar, but for Katania and Christian there was much to learn. George described one incident in which Christian and Katania had surprised and chased a porcupine and another in which Christian had stalked a rhino. The latter was not a sensible idea for a young lion: Christian had crept to within a few yards of the huge beast, the first he had ever seen, before it had spotted him and charged. He must then either have leapt or been thrown high into the air by the outraged rhino. Either way, he dashed past George and fled back to camp, having learned an important life lesson: lions do not tackle full-grown rhinos. Boy, apparently, looked on in scorn.

Sadly, one of these adventures was to lead to the tragic loss of Katania. One morning Christian returned to the camp alone. George was worried: if Boy went off by himself, Christian and Katania would normally stay together. When Boy also returned alone the next day George was seriously concerned and began to search for Katania. His letter explained what he found.

It was not until four days later that I found the spoor of the three lions on the bank of the river. It was plain to see that Christian and Katania had been playing, racing up and down the river bank. I crossed to the far side but found Boy's tracks only. On the near side, there were only the tracks of Christian leaving the river. I think Katania must have tried to follow Boy into the water, but being so much lighter and smaller, would have been carried down by the current. Before she could make the other bank, she was probably taken by a crocodile. Even at her age lions are very good swimmers and it is unlikely she would have drowned. It is a sad loss, which I feel keenly, as do Boy and Christian. The joy has gone out of them.

Letter from George, 12th January 1971

This was a real blow to George's plans to create a pride at Kora. Fortunately, George's friends around Kenya knew that he was looking for females and by June 1971 Boy and Christian had been joined by three lionesses, Juma, Lisa and Mona, together with a young male known as Supercub because of his deep growl.

Meanwhile Boy would sometimes wander off by himself and confront the resident lions, bravely trying to establish his dominance, but these wild lions were tough fighters and Boy often returned to camp with battle scars. The worst was a deep bite on his spine, which George and cameraman Simon Trevor's wife Leila had to treat with hot poultices.

George with Boy beside the Tana river TONY FITZJOHN (GAWPT)

Leila Trevor treats Boy for his spinal injury TONY FITZJOHN (GAWPT)

Tragedy was also to befall Boy. George was concerned that the big lion had been growing increasingly aloof and unfriendly – even towards Christian, with whom he had been inseparable following Katania's death. He wondered whether he might be in permanent pain from his spinal injury. One day, George was having breakfast after his morning walk with the lions, when he heard his assistant Stanley Murithii shouting from the bush outside the compound. Stanley had worked with George for many years and knew Boy well, but on this morning, for reasons we will never know, he broke George's firm rules by leaving camp without permission or an escort. Grabbing his gun, George rushed out of the camp to find Boy with Stanley in his jaws. When Boy saw George, he dropped Stanley and ran off. George had no option but to shoot him. Stanley died before George could get him back to camp.

This double tragedy put the entire rehabilitation programme in danger. Among the people who now criticised George was the distinguished Arabist, traveller and writer Wilfred Thesiger, who wrote a scathing article in the *East African Standard* damning George's rehabilitation project. People remembered the incident in Meru National Park when Boy had attacked young Mark Jenkins. A headline in one of the English tabloids featured a photo of Boy with George under the headline 'Born Free, Died a Killer'.

It was a terrible time for George and he feared that the game department might close down Kampi Ya Simba. Thankfully, he had powerful and influential friends, including former professional hunter Syd Downey, who refuted Thesiger's claims and defused the criticism of George. Only when George was confident that Christian and the other lions were safe did Ace and I fly out to see him and console him about Stanley and Boy. And, of course, we couldn't wait to see Christian.

Christian lying beside Boy's grave TONY FITZJOHN (GAWPT)

George with Christian in the Tana River TONY FITZJOHN (GAWPT)

George with Christian
and the lioness Juma

129

Flying into Kora is always exhilarating. The camp is located in a very remote area of Kenya and for the last hour of the flight there are none of the cultivated patches or gleaming tin roofs that usually betray human habitation. From the moment you sight the Tana River, with its thin green ribbon of doum Palms and riverine forest, you start looking out for Kora Rock and George's Camp.

Terence had planned to extend the landing strip after some pilots had expressed their concerns about its length, but this didn't worry our pilot Heather Stewart, who was an excellent pilot in the mould of the great Kenyan aviatrix Beryl Markham and affectionately known throughout Kenya as 'All-weather Heather'. It wasn't long before we had touched down safely.

When we had called George from Nairobi on the radio telephone, he had warned us that we shouldn't set our expectations too high as he hadn't seen the lions for some weeks. But when he met us at the air strip he was grinning from ear to ear. 'The lions turned up this morning,' he told us. 'Christian must have known you were coming.'

The tragedy of Stanley and Boy was temporarily forgotten in the expectation of our reunion. We were confident that Christian would remember us, and as soon as we reached camp we prepared to set out and find him. George was also confident Christian would remember us. But we had to remind ourselves that he had been in the wild for a year, and – according to George – was well on the way to being totally independent, so we were still hugely apprehensive.

Christian is reunited with John and Ace in a moment that was to captivate millions of viewers on YouTube twenty-seven years later SIMON TREVOR

As Christian greets John, the lioness Mona – barely habituated to humans – approaches to join in the fun SIMON TREVOR

George showed us where to wait, then he went to fetch the lions. This marked a change in the usual routine: George did not generally take visitors to see his lions; they had to wait until the lions wandered into camp. This time, however, he would lead Christian and the two lionesses back towards camp and then over the brow of a rock, from where they could see me, Ace and cameraman Simon Trevor, who had come to film what happened.

As soon as Christian crested the brow of the hill he stopped and stared at us. Then, after a few minutes, he started to walk slowly down the hill towards us, staring the whole time. He looked superb: taller, leaner and less thickly coated than we'd known him, but strong and confident. You could see him wondering who we were, and his body language was self-assured as he approached. He was just making sure it was us. If he had fallen into stalking mode, flattened to the ground and creeping forward, it would have felt very different.

'Call him,' George said, unable to wait any longer.

And that did it: the moment he heard our voices Christian began to run down the rocky hillside, grunting and moaning with excitement. A three-hundred-pound lion was now bounding towards us at about twenty miles per hour; we braced ourselves for the impact. He jumped up to greet us, rubbing our heads, moaning with pleasure and running backwards and forwards between us as he tried to greet us both at the same time.

Not for a moment did either of us think we were in danger, even when the two lionesses arrived to greet us. Mona and Lisa had never really been habituated to humans and had only ever appeared at camp with Christian – yet now, emboldened by Christian's behaviour, they completely accepted us. Today I look at the photographs of my bending down and rubbing heads with Mona and realise how overwhelmed I was by the emotion of the occasion. The gulf between humans and lions had been blurred by sheer euphoria.

The reunion continues

SIMON TREVOR

Following the tragic death of Boy, Christian had been prematurely promoted to head of the pride. In reality, he was far too young for such an alpha position, and Mona and Lisa had already been consorting with a wild lion, known from his tatty appearance as 'Scruffy'. For the next few days we just enjoyed hanging out with Christian when he chose to be with us. We were in his world now and respected his new status – but we were still part of his human pride. This became apparent on one afternoon walk when he suddenly charged into the bushes and chased off Mona and Lisa, who had apparently been waiting to ambush us.

After our brief, achingly short, visit it was appropriate that we left. To stay for too long would have been indulgent and a disruption to Christian's new life. It was a happy farewell, however, as we had seen how magnificently Christian was coping. Indeed, George was telling people that Christian was the easiest lion he was rehabilitating at Kora, despite having started his life in England. It was also heartening to see how fond of Christian George had become and how Christian was helping George cope with the death of Stanley and Boy.

George walking at Kora with Christian and Juma TONY FITZJOHN (GAWPT)

Christian with Juma beside the Tana River TONY FITZJOHN (GAWPT)

9
A FINAL
FAREWELL

In the months following our emotional
reunion with Christian, Tony Fitzjohn
arrived at Kampi Ya Simba. Aged 27,
he was to be the final human player
in the drama of Christian's life. 'I have
been very lucky in finding a young man
to help me,' wrote George. 'A bit of a
wanderer who has tried his hand at many
occupations. Very fit and capable.'

Christian with George, Ace and John
TONY FITZJOHN (GAWPT)

OVERLEAF: **John and Christian during their final days together at Kora in 1972**

TONY FITZJOHN (GAWPT)

Soon after this I received a second letter, again with George's familiar Garissa Post Box address on the back but this time with a new sender's name: Tony Fitzjohn. 'Although we've never met I thought I'd put a few lines together,' wrote Tony. 'I have been helping George for some time and have become as fond of Christian as you must have been. It is amazing to me how he has adapted himself to the wild here yet remains as completely attached to George'.

'Fitz', as he is better known these days, had spent a number of adventurous years travelling around Africa but had always had a hankering to work in Kenya, specifically with George. On his first visit to Kenya, Joy Adamson had offered him a job as her secretary, which he declined, but when he returned in 1971 she had a more interesting offer: "I have nothing going, but I know my husband George is looking for someone," she said. "His previous assistant has just been killed by a lion". (*Born Wild*, Tony Fitzjohn).

Undeterred by such tragic circumstance, Tony grabbed the opportunity and was driven to Kora by Terence where he met Christian and the lionesses Lisa and Juma. Christian was less than welcoming at their first meeting, but George was right, Tony was fit, capable and brave. At their second meeting Tony decided to confront a tail-swishing Christian, walking straight up to him, with a 'Hello, Christian, I'm Fitz.' The reaction was remarkable. 'Christian got up, rubbed his head against me and then just sat there on my feet while I scratched his head. It was the beginning of one of my life's most valuable relationships'. (*Born Wild*, Tony Fitzjohn)

As time passed, Christian came to trust and love Tony. George suggested that perhaps Christian had decided that he came from that same tribe of animals with long hair and odd clothes with whom he had once lived with in London. It was an appealing idea and, whether true or not, the bonding between Christian and Tony was to their mutual advantage: Christian now had another 'minder', and some good company, while Tony had the ideal opportunity to learn about lions with a lion who, although well on the way to self-sufficiency, was still habituated to humans.

Ace and I liked the sound of Tony. Like us, he was clearly coming under Christian's spell. 'You'd be more than proud of Christian now,' he wrote, 'and I'm sure he sends his love, as I send my regards'. Tony had set up a makeshift dark room at Kora – an impressive achievement, using just a 12-volt battery for power – and was regularly sending us photos of the growing Christian.

Thus, in 1972, when Ace and I flew to Kenya to see and find out how Christian was progressing, we were also to meet Tony. He had driven down to Nairobi to meet us and all the way back chatted animatedly about Christian's adventures – and misdemeanours. The lionesses Juma and Lisa had been mating with Scruffy, and had produced a litter of cubs, leaving Christian lonely and frustrated and forcing him to explore across the Tana River. In his boisterous play he had knocked down both George and Tony, but they had both magnanimously credited this atypical behaviour to his loneliness and frustration. George had always maintained that 'teenage' male lions were the most unpredictable.

We already knew there had been confrontations between Christian and the wild lions. George had written to say how was proud he was of Christian's brave stands, noting that his wounds were mostly on his shoulders and forelegs, evidence of Christian's courage. 'Christian had had a fight with a wild lion and had two nasty gashes on his right foreleg,' one letter reported. 'But he did not seem the least perturbed about this and it was with much difficulty that I persuaded him to follow me back to camp, where I could attend to his injuries.'

Christian's adolescent frustrations sometimes led to rough behaviour with George

John with Christian on Kora Rock, enjoying a fine view of the reserve TONY FITZJOHN (GAWPT)

We arrived at camp to find that George had not seen Christian while Tony was away but had heard him mating with a wild lioness. He guessed he was no more than five or six miles away; a lion's roar can travel up to ten miles if the conditions are right. Three days later Christian appeared at Kampi Ya Simba. Did he know we were there? There has been much conjecture about how lions communicate when seemingly out of sight of each other. While hunting they can be observed fanning out over a wide area, yet when one lioness attacks, her sisters are in position to ambush the fleeing target. George had often recounted historic 'coincidences', when he'd found his lions waiting for him at a favourite spot in Meru, sometimes months after he had last paid them a visit.

When Christian strolled casually into camp on the third evening, our first and overwhelming impression was of his size. At only three years old he was still growing, yet George estimated that he already weighed nearly five hundred pounds. How could Juma and Lisa have preferred Scruffy to this magnificent specimen? It must surely be down to 'experience', as in lion years Christian was still a teenager.

He was as vocal as ever with his greetings, though the grunts were deeper, and he pushed and shoved as he rubbed himself against us in his excitement. George was knocked right off his chair, spilling his precious White Horse Whiskey, which did not amuse him. Christian greeted us all in rotation, from George to Ace to me – and to Tony, of whom we could see for the first time how fond he was.

That evening we rather over-celebrated, and even Christian looked exhausted the next morning. When we went for a walk he soon settled down under a cool rocky overhang, where he would spend the rest of the day with the lionesses – who grimaced at the human smell that he had acquired by spending time with us. For the next eight days, we either walked with Christian or just sat beside him on his favourite rocks overlooking the camp. It seemed he was maturing fast, and was no longer the playful cub or even the exuberant teenager who had jumped on George and Tony.

At three years old, Christian had become far too heavy for anybody's lap TONY FITZJOHN (GAWPT)

LEFT: Christian jumps up on George's Land Rover during what was to be his last meeting with John and Ace TONY FITZJOHN (GAWPT)

BELOW: The back window of George's Land Rover allows a final view of Christian JOHN RENDALL

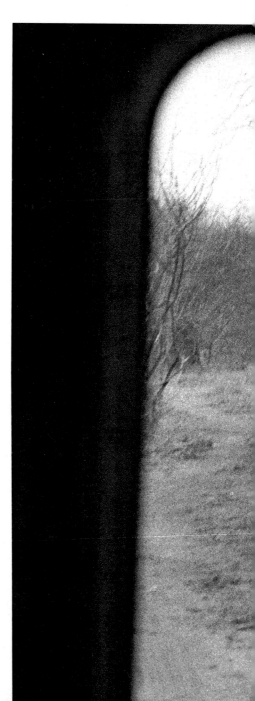

On our last day, we drove out to find Christian and say goodbye. We didn't know for certain that this would be our final farewell but we somehow suspected it. When we found him, he jumped up to greet us and climbed onto the Land Rover, rubbing heads and making that wonderful familiar grunt. Finally, he jumped down. As we drove away he trotted behind us for a while, but only half-heartedly. It was a quiet drive back to camp, and a subdued return journey to Nairobi.

10
CHRISTIAN'S NEW WORLD

When Ace and I first met Joy in 1970, she was both critical and dubious about Christian's chances of survival. She reminded us that Elsa had been born in Africa, and knew sounds and smells. And she didn't mince her words about the dangers. 'Your stupid fat lion will be killed,' she said. 'And so will George'.

I had to admit that Joy was right about Christian's ignorance of life in the wild. It was true that he was over-sized and overweight for his age – but that was only because we had cared for him so well and he had been fed so regularly; no lion cub in the wild would enjoy four meals a day. But he was fit and, what's more, he was trusting of human beings, an essential factor in rehabilitation.

George with Christian on the rocks at Kora
TONY FITZJOHN (GAWPT)

Our disconcerting conversation with Joy was held in the sitting room of Elsamere, her house on Lake Naivasha bought with the profits from *Born Free*. It was a superb location, with lawns running down to the lake and black-and-white colobus monkeys playing in the trees, but the lion skin upholstery on the sofas was rather disconcerting. 'There are good lions and there are bad lions,' said Joy, when I ventured that I was not very comfortable sitting on lion skins. 'George had to shoot the bad ones.'

Eventually I realised that the real reason for Joy's cynicism about Christian was that it gave George a reason for leaving Elsamere and returning to the bush he so loved. While Boy was recovering, George had been living in a simple cottage in the grounds beside his compound. Joy's paying visitors had been taken to see the man and his lion, almost as though they were exhibits.

Joy had frustrations of her own. Following a car accident in which she had damaged her right hand, she could no longer play the piano or paint – which was a setback for such a talented musician and artist. And though she had begun painting with her left hand, these paintings could not match the brilliance of her earlier botanical paintings nor those published in her book *Peoples of Kenya*. It was also unfeasible that she could continue her field work by living in remote areas. It thus enraged her that George had suddenly gained a new lease of life with this new project. She was determined that Christian could not be successfully rehabilitated, and her anger unjustly focused on Bill Travers, who was producing the documentary about the process.

ABOVE and OPPOSITE: **Joy Adamson with Christian**
TONY FITZJOHN (GAWPT)

But eventually, just as he had done before with many other doubters, Christian won Joy's admiration. Eighteen months after our uncomfortable meeting with her, I was amused to see a series of photographs sent by Tony Fitzjohn, showing Joy with Christian. She had insisted on being photographed with her arms around the patient lion. It was a relief finally to have Joy's acknowledgement that Christian had 'grown into a fine young lion'. No one could resist Christian.

Joy particularly loved the idea that Christian's mother Mary had come from Rotterdam Zoo and may have been related to Elsa's sisters 'Big One'

and 'Lustica', a fact I had forgotten to mention when I first met her. Had I done so, perhaps she might have been more supportive at that first meeting.

Back at Kora, as Christian became more and more independent of George, he sought to establish his own territory and visited the camp less and less. George and Tony often heard him roaring his challenges to resident lions and, more than once heard the telltale noises of him mating. Although these wild lionesses were never sighted, nor any cubs, George was confident that Christian had successfully passed on his genes.

Christian with Joy (above) and George Adamson (opposite)
TONY FITZJOHN (GAWPT)

George had been counting the days since Christian's last visit to Kampi Ya Simba. After ninety-seven days, he stopped. He knew by then that Christian would not be coming back. Both George and Tony Fitzjohn felt Christian's absence keenly, but they also knew that the young lion's departure meant that their hard work had been a success. 'Christian had been so much part of our lives … that we all felt a deep sense of sadness and loss,' wrote George (*My Pride and Joy*), 'yet I was almost equally happy that he was exercising his freedom in a way that was wise'.

In early 1974, after George wrote to say that Christian had disappeared into the wild, I decided to visit him and Tony at Kampi Ya Simba. Even if I couldn't find Christian, I would at least meet the new lions that George and Tony were rehabilitating. Ace was in America but I had some time to travel.

When I arrived, I found the camp now well established. Terence had completed more huts, using his simple proven construction methods: cement-painted hessian over chicken wire for the walls and woven palm leaves (*makuti*) for the roofing, all supported by mangrove poles. With the exception of chicken wire and nail, it was an effective and an economical use of local materials. There were also more kerosene deep freezes, for storing camel meat for the lions, although the only means of communication with the outside world was still the radio telephone.

George Adamson with Christian TONY FITZJOHN (GAWPT)

To hear George's stories about Christian and his adventures was such a pleasure. George may have been an excellent correspondent but he was an even better raconteur, particularly after dinner with a glass of his favourite White Horse whisky, and he was always happy to talk about Christian.

George recounted one incident in 1973 when Christian had returned for a few days and was sitting with George and Tony on the banks of the Tana. The young lion suddenly stood up and stared intently at the river. Through their binoculars, George and Tony could only see what looked like a couple of floating logs. On closer scrutiny, however, these turned out to be an upturned canoe and bedding. No wonder Christian had been intrigued! The gear belonged to a group from the World Bank – hailing from Greece, Scotland and Japan – who had been attempting to canoe down the Tana when one had capsized. On sighting George and Tony, one began to cross the river, but his safari preparations had obviously not included a warning about crocodiles and he was firmly instructed to wait on the other side until George came to rescue him and his party.

Safely ensconced back at Kampi Ya Simba the following day, the group was very alarmed when Christian casually strolled into camp. George quickly calmed them when he explained that had it not been for Christian's keen eyesight they might never have been found. They were convinced that they owed their survival to him.

During this trip, Tony and I made a half-hearted attempt to find Christian on the other side of the Tana River but didn't really expect any success. 'Christian had gone forever,' Tony later wrote in *Born Wild*. 'He had moved from a Bentley in Chelsea to a Land Rover in Kora and now he had gone off to Meru, where they had new Toyotas, to start his own lineage. We were proud of him but, God, I missed him'.

George, also, no longer realistically expected a visit from Christian, now that he had crossed the Tana.

He knew that the young lion would be busy fighting off the challenges of other resident lions, whose roars George had heard, and that a return journey to camp would necessitate passing back through this occupied territory and leaving behind any hard-fought-for lionesses he had acquired on the other side.

Ours was thus a self-indulgent search. But it was, at least, an opportunity to assess game numbers on the other side of the river and to see whether there were any illegal cattle grazers in the area. One morning we drove out into an open area where a tower (herd) of giraffe were grazing on the fringing acacia bushes. There seemed to be something distinctly odd about them – and we soon realized that one was an albino. Neither Tony nor I had ever seen such an animal – but in our excitement, we were unable to get out a camera out before it disappeared into the bush. On that side of the Tana the game was extremely shy, as Somali herders with their livestock were regular visitors, so we couldn't track the giraffe any further.

After a few days, with no sightings of Christian or any lion spoor, we reluctantly returned to camp. I was disappointed, yes, but I accepted the fact that Christian had disappeared into the wild forever. He had his new hunting grounds. He no longer needed me, or Ace, or the rest of his human pride back in London. Now he didn't even need George or Tony.

We were confident Christian had survived. George had taught him to keep away from people and cattle, and there were never any reports of a large lion having been poached or shot. (Christian would have been the largest lion in the area, and an exceptional trophy attracts attention and gossip.) In 1978, a lion called Kaunda that George had rehabilitated was seen on the boundary of Meru National Park, where he was successfully living in the wild. This served to bolster George's confidence that Christian, too, had found his way to these richer hunting grounds.

All in all, it was the perfect rehabilitation.

Christian's remarkable story was in stark contrast to that of his sister Martha, who we had last seen in Harrods on the day we collected him. We later discovered that Martha had been purchased with a cheque that had 'bounced' – something that often happened before the days of cheque guarantee cards. By the time the police caught the man responsible he had already sold Martha. The lion was never found, and the man was jailed for theft. From prison, he wrote the following letter to Roy Hazle, the chief buyer at Harrods Zoo.

26th December 1969
H.M. Prison Brixton London W2
Dear Sir,
I have been told that you and the young lady (a reference to Sandy Lloyd) *that works with you have been worried about the lion cub I got from you. May I put your mind at rest and tell you that it is now in a very nice home. It has a very nice shed which is heated and a big garden to play in. Two nice girls are looking after it, as it is the family pet. It gets the best of food to live on .... a dozen eggs and fresh milk every day and plenty of meat. It's in the home of a film star. So please don't worry about it and tell the lady who used to look after it that it could not get a better home. This will give her a little comfort because I know she liked her very much so please don't worry it's being well looked after.*
Yours sincerely
J. R. Styles

Could this be true? Martha living with a film star as a family pet? It all sounded rather fanciful, and my letters to Mr Styles asking for more details went unanswered, so Martha effectively vanished.

Or did she? In July 1971, Sandy Lloyd spotted an advertisement in the 'Animals for Sale' section of *Cage and Aviary Birds* magazine. '*Two-year-old tame hand-reared Lioness. Beautiful condition, to g home. Box 75 CB*'. Excited, she rang me immediately. I called the publication to ask whether they could supply more details of the advertiser and, after much persuasion, they disclosed that it was a Mr R Dewhurst, at an address in Long Bennington,

George Adamson with Christian
TONY FITZJOHN (GAWPT)

Newark, Nottinghamshire. I dashed off a letter offering to buy the lioness. A week later my letter was returned unopened with 'Gone away' scribbled on the envelope. I rang the police to ask whether they would visit the farm and see whether there was, in fact, a lioness for sale. They confirmed that a Mr Dewhurst had indeed 'gone away' but that there was no sign of a lioness. They were not prepared to make any further enquiries.

Could it have been Martha? Certainly, she would have been the right age. How wonderful it would have been if we had been able to reunite her with Christian.

11
GEORGE'S MURDER

By 1989, George and Tony had
successfully rehabilitated nearly thirty
lions, living frugally and relying on
donors and generous friends for financial
support. There was never any spare cash
for luxuries, sometimes not even enough
for essentials, but the lions were always
fed. Tony has never had a salary, but
visitors helped out and brought supplies,
and George had the modest royalties
from his books.

George Adamson with Christian
TONY FITZJOHN (GAWPT)

I was always impressed by George's gracious acceptance of Joy's financial success. He never complained that she did not share the considerable income she received from the book *Born Free*, or from the subsequent film, or that her Elsa Trust charity funded projects all over the world, but never George's work at Kora.

Joy never divorced George, despite often talking about it, and the two remained friends – albeit largely at a distance – for the rest of their lives. Joy occasionally visited from her home, Elsamere, on Lake Naivasha. She did not approve of Tony, despite having originally recommended him to George, and disliked Terence, so whenever she visited Kora, Tony and Terence had to move out of camp.

Joy was murdered in 1980 at her camp in Shaba National Park, where she had rehabilitated her cheetah Pippa and leopard Penny. One of her former employees, a young Turkana named Paul Ekai, was charged and sentenced for the murder. Today, out of jail and living near Isiolo, he still maintains his innocence. His conviction, he claims, was made on the basis of a confession that was tortured out of him by the police. Joy's death was international news at the time, and once the erroneous suggestion that she had been killed by a lion had been discredited, the government wanted a culprit as soon as possible. Ekai fitted the bill: he had recently been fired by Joy and they had argued over a missing camera and his pay.

Unfortunately, Joy never had George's ability to work comfortably with local employees, and any number of the people she had sacked or shouted at over the years might have harboured a murderous grudge against her. Even her young European assistant, Pieter Mawson, with whom she also frequently and publicly argued, had initially been considered a possible suspect. He was cleared and soon after left for South Africa, where he later died in a car accident.

Joy Adamson's death was one of a number of high-profile murder cases in Kenya – from Lord Erroll of *White Mischief* notoriety and the young English girl Julie Ward, to conservationist and film-maker Joan Root, artist Tonio Trebinski and, more recently, young Alexander Monson and the anti-ivory trade activist Esmond Bradley Martin – in which the perpetrator of the crime has never been established beyond doubt. People are charged but witnesses disappear, evidence is lost, cases drag on for years and no satisfactory solution is reached. Paul Ekai may well be innocent of Joy's murder. When Virginia McKenna spoke to

him after his release, she left the meeting seriously wondering whether he may have been innocent.

George suffered another personal loss in 1986, when his brother Terence died at Kora. This tough, cantankerous and laconic old man had owned only one suit all his life (which he kept for weddings and funerals, and stored in a welded-up chest), and was buried on the banks of the Tana beside one of the lions, Supercub. Terence had played a vital role at Kora, initially clearing tracks and building Kampi Ya Simba and then opting to stay with George for 15 years, with only rare visits to his home in Malindi. At

Kora the problems with Somali herders with their cattle, goats and camels had steadily increased over the years, and George and Tony had resorted to sleeping in trenches, guns by their side. George's vulnerability was further increased when Tony was forced to leave after spurious charges were made against him regarding gun licences. The authorities wanted George out of Kora and they assumed that by removing Tony, he would have to follow. They were wrong: George would not leave Kampi Ya Simba and his lions. And his obstinacy had tragic results.

Drawing of George Adamson with Christian and Boy, by artist Gary Hodges
GARY HODGES, BORN FREE FOUNDATION

On 20th August 1989, George was murdered at Kora by *shifta*, the Somali bandits who roamed much of northern Kenya. It happened when the general service unit that had been providing camp security were away dealing with poaching and bandit activity elsewhere. George, aware of the danger, had asked his guests to leave. All but one, a German lady called Inge Ledeheil, had done so.

When an unexpected plane buzzed the camp that morning, George prepared to collect the arrivals. This was the normal process when arriving at Kora: buzz the camp, land and wait to be collected. A sign at the airstrip warned guests that lions could be in the area and that arrivals should wait in the plane until George arrived. On this day, to save George the trip, Inge offered to go to the strip. She took with her Bitacha, one of the camp staff. Soon after they had left camp, George heard shots. He realised immediately that Inge and Bitacha had been attacked.

George did not have a large armoury to defend himself, but grabbing his pistol and more staff, he jumped in the Land Rover and sped towards the sound of firing. When he arrived at the scene, he saw that Bitacha had been wounded and that Inge was being dragged into the bushes. Without hesitation, he drove straight at the attackers, firing his pistol. Hopelessly outgunned, he and two of his staff were killed, cut down in a hail of machine-gun fire.

It was a heroic death; a death that shocked people all over Kenya and the world. And it posed a huge public relations problem for the Kenyan government. How could the most famous conservationist in Kenya – a man whose wife had also been murdered – be left unguarded, to be murdered by bandits?

The first news of the murder came via a friend of George's, Jane McKeand, who ran a private 'ham' radio station at Laikipia, to which George had regularly contributed. Jane had been contacted from Kampi ya Simba by a frightened member of

George's unique understanding of lions allowed him to develop close bonds with both **Boy and Christian** TONY FITZJOHN (GAWPT)

George's staff who was unfamiliar with the radio telephone and had been struggling for some hours to make it work. She immediately contacted Richard Leakey, the new head of Kenya Wildlife Services, who knew George well and recognised what a public relations disaster this had created.

Hardest hit by the tragedy was Tony Fitzjohn, who had feared something like this would happen but was unable to defend George from his new base at Mkomazi in Tanzania. When George was buried beside Terence and Supercub on the banks of the Tana, however, Tony was not allowed to speak at the funeral. Perhaps this was due to official embarrassment – an implicit acknowledgement that George's death had become almost inevitable once Tony had been forced to leave Kora. It was Tony who

had made it possible for George to stay at Kora, becoming his surrogate son. He was the obvious successor, but self-interested people were unwilling to support what had clearly been George's hope.

Many of George's true friends had flown to Kora for the funeral, including Bill Travers and Virginia McKenna, and I always regret that I was unable to travel from Australia. There were others there, however, including the Game Department rangers and other government officials, who had done nothing to help protect George after Tony had been forced to leave. Film footage shows these smartly uniformed individuals providing a self-important guard of honour for the 'Old Man', with no apparent sense of irony. With many press in attendance, however, Richard Leakey used the eulogy to

John stands beside George Adamson's grave at Kora TANIA HITCHINS

The battered door of the Land Rover in which George was murdered

JOHN RENDALL

publicise his stand on poaching. He made it clear that in future poachers would be shot and that Kora would henceforth be gazetted and policed as a national park.

Over the years since the funeral, the three graves on the banks of the Tana have been repeatedly disturbed and the headstones damaged by Somali herdsmen illegally grazing their stock, but the George Adamson Trust or others have always repaired them. The latest headstones are not entirely accurate – Supercub's grave is labelled as Boy's; Boy is, in fact, buried closer to Kampi Ya Simba – but I hope, nonetheless, that they will remain intact.

With George dead, and Tony banned from Kora and committed to his fledgling project at Mkomazi in the name of the George Adamson Wildlife Preservation Trust, Kora was effectively abandoned. Though now gazetted as a national park, thanks to

Richard Leakey, its guiding spirit had been murdered and his chosen successor banished.

With Tony, I did attend George's memorial service in St James Church on Piccadilly in London. As at Kora, Tony was not invited to speak, but after the service the great and the good of the conservation world – together with George's friends in the UK – gathered around to console him and to add their support for the George Adamson Wildlife Preservation Trust. Originally called the Kora Wildlife Preservation Trust, George had requested that it be renamed and its scope extended so that future projects in his name would not be confined to Kora.

By 1989, Christian would also have been dead. Lions can live for twenty years in captivity, but twelve or fourteen years is a good life in the wild. We all hoped that Christian's progeny would survive without George and Tony there to protect them.

12
MKOMAZI

Before his death, George Adamson had wanted to ensure that Tony Fitzjohn would receive support in any other future conservation projects beyond Kora. In turn, as Field Director of the George Adamson Wildlife Preservation Trust, Tony was determined to perpetuate George's dream of an Africa where wildlife could roam freely in wild and natural areas. If it couldn't be at Kora, or elsewhere in Kenya, it could be in Tanzania, at Mkomazi.

The first four black rhinos arrive at Mkomazi from Addo Elephant
National Park, South Africa JOHN RENDALL

The core founding trustees of the George Adamson Wildlife Preservation Trust were Tony's fellow students from his alma mater, the prestigious Mill Hill School in London: Bob Marshall-Andrews, Andy Mortimer, Allan Toulson and Peter Wakeman, plus Anthony Marrian (an old friend of Tony's from Kenya). The first Chairman was distinguished Cambridge University zoologist Dr Keith Eltringham. Other initial supporters included people who had worked with George, had known him or had visited him at Kora. Some had never had any direct contact with him but simply wished to see his work carried on. This eclectic group enthusiastically supported the Trust and became 'Friends', regularly donating money to cover the cost of running Tony's new projects in Tanzania.

The Mkomazi Game Reserve in northern Tanzania is an area of one thousand, two hundred square miles that, by the time of Tony's arrival in 1988, had suffered from years of neglect. With little funding, poor management, endemic poaching, random burning, illegal hunting and over-grazing, the reserve was so severely degraded that the Tanzanian government had even considered de-gazetting it. Fortunately, however, they had a change of policy and declared Mkomazi a National Priority Project. Tony was invited to oversee the rehabilitation of the whole reserve, with the stipulation that he re-establish the African wild dog and the black rhino, two highly endangered species once found on the reserve but since poached and hunted to extinction.

The project brought huge challenges for Tony and the new Trust. The first progress came with the wild dog breeding programme, thanks to the dedication of Dutch veterinarian Dr Aart Visee from the African Wild Dog Foundation. Wild dogs have a poor reputation with cattle herders and farmers, who consider them vermin to be poisoned or shot, but they have a vital role to play in the balance of wildlife numbers, weeding out the old or sick animals and dispersing herds, thus limiting inbreeding.

Tony Fitzjohn uses a blowpipe to inoculate the wild dogs at Mkomazi JOHN RENDALL

Innocent Killers, the classic 1970 book by Hugo and Jane Van Lawick-Goodall, provides an excellent account of the lives of these sociable animals and their role in a balanced ecosystem. Aart inoculated the dogs against rabies and canine distemper, helping to produce healthier individuals for reintroduction into the wild.

The cost of the wild dog enclosures at Mkomazi was manageable, but the huge cost of fencing a rhino sanctuary, with miles of poles and wire, posed a much greater challenge. This second phase of the rehabilitation programme at Mkomazi was to take far longer, and required a considerably higher investment. Dams had to be built and, because elephants had stopped visiting Mkomazi, the natural water holes had become clogged so had to be cleared and opened up. Without elephants maintaining water holes, there is less water for the other game. A mechanical elephant was thus supplied, courtesy of

Sir Anthony (now Lord) Bamford of JCB, who continues to be a generous supporter, supplying spares and new equipment. Access roads were surveyed and graded, and the fencing of the initially twenty-five square mile rhino sanctuary – by far the costliest part of the project – got under way. It was to take ten years of hard work and fund raising before the sanctuary was finished, and the first rhinos could arrive from Addo Elephant National Park in South Africa.

In the 1970s, when I first visited Tanzania, there were an estimated seven thousand black rhinos in the country, including possibly two hundred and fifty at Mkomazi. By 1997, this number had plummeted, with none at Mkomazi and fewer than two hundred in the whole of Tanzania. The demand for rhino horn in the markets of the far east – based on a myth that this hair-like substance possesses either medicinal or aphrodisiac qualities – had led to a catastrophic population collapse in just thirty years.

Veterinarian Pete Morkel oversees the unloading of the black rhinos from the Antanov JOHN RENDALL

The four rhinos being imported from Addo were descendants of those taken by road from Tanzania in the 1960s. This new generation would be arriving in a chartered Russian-built Antanov, however, and the Mkomazi airstrip had to be extended to accommodate the giant aircraft. The George Adamson Trust purchased the rhinos from the South African Parks Board, which was selling them because they were not indigenous to the Addo area. Recognising the importance of re-establishing the black rhino at Mkomazi, the board gave the Trust very favourable terms. Indeed, this was surely the first time that rhinos anywhere had been acquired by hire purchase!

The return of rhinos to Mkomazi generated great excitement among all involved, from the supporters of the George Adamson Trust to the staff at Mkomazi, local residents, government officials and Tanzanian wildlife personnel. On the big day, a party of dignitaries travelled to the reserve, and a British television production company, HIT Entertainment, arrived to make a documentary about the event and the work of the George Adamson Wildlife Preservation Trust. There was a festive atmosphere on the airstrip as we waited for the Antanov to land.

The celebrations and filming were delayed, however, because the Russian pilots had not been able to find the landing strip at Mkomazi so had landed at Kilimanjaro International Airport some ninety miles away. Tourists arriving on a KLM charter flight at Kilimanjaro were apparently rather alarmed when they saw the Antanov touching down, with its ominous – though redundant – gun turrets. There was also great interest when Veterinarian Pete Morkel and the two South African rangers travelling with the rhinos began collecting browse for the animals from around the airstrip.

The landing gear of the Antanov bogged down on the landing strip

JOHN RENDALL

Pete was not happy about waiting at Kilimanjaro for too long, so Tony flew to Kilimanjaro in his Cessna to meet the Russian pilots and offered to lead them back to Mkomazi. He explained that the far end of the runway was rather soft and muddy so suggested they should fly over the strip first, to allow them to assess where best to touch down. All now seemed back on course: Tony landed and we watched the Antanov approach the landing strip for its reconnoitering flypast. But, to our surprise, the pilot decided to land immediately – and way too far up the runway. The official welcoming party had to dash for safety as the giant aircraft tore up the strip, mud flying. Thankfully the pilot managed to slew around to a stop, perilously close to the end of the runway and a small rocky outcrop from where I was filming.

'I hate rhinos and I hate Fitzjohn!' shouted the shaken – but grinning – Russian pilot as he stepped down from the aircraft. We congratulated him on his 'wonderful landing'. At last, the rhinos were home. There were huge sighs of relief. Perversely, the dramatic landing made excellent footage for the documentary, adding to the general excitement of the event. *Mkomazi: The Return of the Rhino* recorded the momentous day, with a narration from the distinguished actor Edward Fox, and helped to publicise the work of the Trust to an international audience.

The first four rhinos flourished in their new home. The two males, James and Jonah, were subsequently fitted with microchips so that they could be tracked around the sanctuary. Again, it was veterinarian Pete Morkel who oversaw this risky and highly skilled process, using a dart gun to sedate the rhinos from a helicopter before dropping down beside the anaesthetized beasts to link up with the ground crew. The team drilled into the horn, inserted the chip and filled up the hole with resin – all as quickly as possible, before the rhino overheated.

Tony and his staff were now able to keep constant tabs on their rhinos. And in 2010 the rhino gene pool was expanded when three rhino arrived from an unlikely source, the Dvur Kralove Zoo in Czechoslovakia. The challenge of the

The rhino holding boma at Mkomazi JOHN RENDALL

major international transport cost was met by the enthusiastic and generous Suzuki Rhino Club in Holland who were already helping fund the security of the Rhino Sanctuary. Suzuki sell a popular model called the 'Rhino' so it was a symbiotic relationship between Suzuki Holland and the Trust and as Christian's mother Mary had come from Holland it was another co-incidental Dutch-Adamson Trust link.

In 2012, the gene pool was further expanded when three black rhinos from the UK arrived at Kilimanjaro International Airport. These had been donated by the Aspinall Foundation, named after the late John Aspinall, who bred endangered species at

his private wild animal parks in Kent, Port Lympne and Howletts. Aspinall's son Damian has continued in his father's footsteps, maintaining precious gene pools of such endangered species as gorilla, tiger, black rhino and bongo, and facilitating the rehabilitation of certain species back into the wild.

Funding for the transport of the Aspinall rhinos to Tanzania was secured when Charlie Mayhew, Chief Executive of the Tusk Trust, asked the international transport company DHL to sponsor the flight. Their generous agreement made the translocation possible. The Patron of Tusk Trust, HRH The Duke of Cambridge, visited Port Lympne to see the rhinos

destined for Mkomazi and took the opportunity to speak to the press about the devastating impact of poaching. 'Stamping out the illegal wildlife trade needs to be placed very near the top of the global agenda,' said Prince William, while supporting his father Prince Charles at the Wildlife Trade Conference in 2103. 'It needs to be addressed by world leaders as an urgent priority'.

Somehow, during all this activity at Mkomazi, Tony found time to write his autobiography, *Born Wild*, and to advise with the filming of his life story, *To Walk with Lions*, in which Richard Harris played George and Honor Blackman played a far more true-to-life Joy than Virginia McKenna's version in *Born Free*. Guests of honour at the London premiere of the film were Princess Michael of Kent, Patron of the George Adamson Wildlife Preservation Trust, and her husband Prince Michael, who have regularly visited Mkomazi to see the rhino breeding programme. George's friends in attendance were slightly unnerved by Richard Harris's superb performance. Even George's old nemesis Wilfred Thesiger came. The great writer, who had so fiercely criticised George's work with lions when Boy had attacked young Mark Jenkins, congratulated Harris on his portrayal of George.

All this publicity drew attention to the success of the rehabilitation programmes and helped gain official recognition of the work of the George Adamson Trust. Mkomazi was upgraded from reserve to a national park and, in 2006, Tony Fitzjohn was awarded an OBE for his services to conservation. Today Mkomazi is recognised as one of the most successful conservation projects in Africa. Both the rhinos and the wild dogs are breeding successfully, and Tony and his team are rightly proud of their success. There is no doubt that George Adamson would have approved.

ABOVE: **James, one of the four translocated black rhinos, inside the holding boma**

JOHN RENDALL

Tony Fitzjohn with the Mkomazi wild dog pack JOHN RENDALL

13
SEARCHING FOR SIGNS OF CHRISTIAN

Since 2012, I have had the good fortune of escorting safaris to Kenya. My trips have focused on the Northern Frontier Department, where George Adamson was working as a game ranger while he and Joy raised Elsa, and to Kora, to see where Christian was rehabilitated and visit the rock where our 1971 reunion took place.

The wild terrain of Meru National Park, northern Kenya, where Christian's descendants may still be roaming free

MIKE UNWIN

The focal point in Meru National Park is Elsa's Kopje Lodge, which is built on the rocky outcrop above the site where George and Joy had their first camp and had begun Elsa's rehabilitation. One of the best lodges in Africa, it is virtually invisible from the air, its organic materials of rock, wood, thatch and woven palm nestling seamlessly into the hillside, with only the swimming pool to give it away.

This lodge is also the closest to Kampi Ya Simba and Kora. To get there by road takes an arduous seven-hour slog in a four-wheel-drive vehicle, but it is a mere forty-minute flight to the airstrip built by George's brother Terence. Tony Fitzjohn has rebuilt the camp, which was abandoned after George's murder in 1989. Today it is a perfect facsimile of the original, albeit with a large satellite dish for internet contact – a major upgrade on the primitive wireless radio that was the only way of contacting the outside world when the camp was built in 1970.

Sadly, I never saw any lions during my visits to Kora: Somali herdsmen with their cattle, camels and goats now regularly cross the Tana River and they have either poached or poisoned much of the game. Where once there were lion, rhino, elephant, zebra, waterbuck, giraffe and kudu, there are now only herds of livestock grazing illegally.

It is doubtful whether Christian's descendants, and those of the other thirty lions George rehabilitated, would have survived had they stayed at Kora. But the prospects would have been better for any that followed Christian's route to the safety of the adjoining Meru National Park. The lions in this Northern Frontier Department area are mostly arid-country lions with small manes, but Philip Mason, the astute manager of Elsa's Kopje, has occasionally seen big-maned individuals that more resemble Christian. 'I believe a bit of World's End in Chelsea is at the end of the world here,' he has commented. If Philip is right, it suggests that Christian's genes may have been perpetuated just as George always believed they were.

Today, Elsa's Kopje Lodge offers an upmarket safari experience to visitors from around the world ELEWANA

A photo of George hangs in the rebuilt Kampi ya Simba, Kora JOHN RENDALL

Visitors to Meru today can enjoy fine views of Elsa's Kopje; the reserve's abundant wildlife includes zebra (above left), shy lesser kudu (top right) and birds such as white-throated bee-eater (above right) MIKE UNWIN

On a game drive with guests in 2012, Richard Morogo – one of the rangers at Elsa's Kopje – found a lioness with two cubs. The lioness was mature and healthy, but the cubs were from different litters: one possibly eighteen months old, with the first hint of a dark, Christian-like, mane; the other a smaller cub just a few months old. The following day, Richard found that the lioness and the elder cub had left, presumably to hunt, leaving the small cub safely hidden under a rock overhang. There was nothing unusual about this, but two days later, when Richard checked again, he found the small cub still alone and starting to show signs of distress. After two further days passed without the lioness returning, the cub was in real trouble.

The powerful build of this
lioness at Meru today
suggests that she may
possibly have some of
Christian's inheritance in
her genes MIKE UNWIN

Philip Mason spoke to Kenya Wildlife Services in Nairobi and asked whether he could rescue the cub. As a rule, wildlife cannot be removed from national parks and staff are not allowed to interfere with the natural processes of life and death, but Philip was persuasive. This cub appeared to have been abandoned – perhaps the mother had been injured or chased away by other lions – and, what's more, it was in 'Adamson territory'. Philip and Richard were surprised and delighted to find that KWS were sympathetic to the proposal, perhaps swayed by the Adamson connection. They retrieved the weakened, dehydrated cub and rushed him down to the Nairobi Orphanage at Nairobi National Park.

Could this cub, which had now been named Richard, be related to Christian? On my next visit to Kenya, my first stop was at the orphanage. I was introduced to the cub by Chyssie Bradley-Martin, who has spent many years assisting there. Richard was a fine young lion, about five months old at that stage, and he certainly bore a similarity to Christian at the same age. I found him sharing a compound with two other orphaned lion cubs and, because of a shortage of space, a young serval cat and a leopard. All were playing happily together.

Chryssie and I collected some DNA samples from a rather unwilling Richard, and I brought these back to England to see whether we could establish a link to Christian. I still had Christian's lead, while Christian's surrogate mother Jennifer-Mary Taylor has a fur coat Christian often slept on, so we were optimistic. Unfortunately, Christian's DNA could not be established from either of these items. Any connection between Christian and Richard thus remains conjecture.

I had hoped that the orphanage would offer all three cubs to Tony Fitzjohn for Kora but the timing wasn't right and the cubs remained there. On my last visit, Richard had been renamed Godfrey after his new keeper. He was nearly two-and-a-half years old and looked even more like Christian.

Sadly, it seems Godfrey will spend the rest of his life at the orphanage. He is too old to be rehabilitated, and is not habituated to humans so it would be impossible to keep him under observation if he were returned to the wild. If there is one thing that George Adamson proved through his work, it is that lions can't simply be let loose. He often wrote that his greatest successes were with Elsa and Christian, who were the most habituated of all his lions.

In the orphanage at Nairobi National Park, three lion cubs share an enclosure with a young leopard and a young serval; the large cub in the centre may possibly be a descendant of Christian JOHN RENDALL

POSTSCRIPT

We all had a lot to thank Christian for

Tony Fitzjohn
From *Born Wild: The Extraordinary Story of One Man's Passion for Lions and for Africa*, Tony Fitzjohn,
first published Viking 2010

A YOUTUBE SENSATION

In 2006, a young American art student named Lisa Williams was researching a college project and scanning the internet for inspiration, when she stumbled across a clip from our 1971 television documentary, *A Lion Called Christian*. The sequence, filmed by leading wildlife cameramen Simon Trevor, showed our reunion with Christian after he had been living in the wild for over a year. When I met Lisa, years later, she explained how she had found the clip on a Japanese blog site and that, although it had no soundtrack, commentary or explanation, she was so intrigued that she posted it on her personal blog.

One of the bloggers who saw Lisa's clip was a young English actor named Marc Bolton. He was inspired to add a commentary and a sound track, using the emotive Whitney Houston song *I will Always Love You*. In the original film, *The Lion from World's End*, the group Pentangle had provided the music. Although charming, this does not match the passion in Whitney's voice, which lifts the sequence to a much more emotional level. The jazz singer Madeleine Bell had originally sung her song, *This is the story of Christian the Lion*, but the film company had rejected it as too racy. Ironically, this recording was much closer in its emotional intensity to the more famous song recorded by Whitney.

The first time I became aware of the clip's existence was when a friend rang to tell me that they had seen film of two long-haired young men with a lion. As we had once had a lion, they thought I might be interested. 'That's us! That's Christian!' I said, calling back immediately I'd seen it for myself. 'How did that happen?'

For many years I had been using the original film, which includes this sequence, in talks at schools and to groups of conservationists, but I had never thought of creating a YouTube clip – indeed, I hadn't the slightest idea of how to do so! I consulted a lawyer about the apparent copyright infringement and the possibility of the clip generating revenue for the George Adamson Trust. He believed that it was too late to 'claim' the clip because over 600,000 people had already seen it, and that 'there probably wouldn't be many more hits'.

After American chat show host Ellen DeGeneres showed the clip on her programme, however, the number of viewings shot up to over three million. I again consulted the lawyer, who did have the decency to apologise but thought that three million really was as high as it would go. How wrong he was! Today there have been over 100 million viewings. I can only imagine how much money that might have generated for the Trust.

On the positive side, all this publicity created the impetus for us to republish our book: the second edition of *A Lion Called Christian* was published in over 25 international editions, so people all over the world now know about Christian. The YouTube clip also leads viewers on to other conservation clips and issues. Christian has thus become an ambassador for conservation, helping increase awareness of the current crisis facing lions and many other species. On the back of Christian's story, both Ace and I have been able to talk to numerous different groups all over the world about conservation issues.

The YouTube clip also led to the production of a television documentary, *The Lion Cub from Harrods*, which traces the phenomenal interest in Christian generated by the reunion sequence. One of the many bonuses filming this was a meeting with Lisa Williams in Los Angeles. Unfortunately, I had still not met Marc Bolton when the documentary was made, so we were unable to give him the credit he deserves. Since then, however, I finally tracked Marc down, and he kindly explained how he came to make the clip.

The pivotal moment in the YouTube reunion clip that has drawn more than 100 million viewings to date

SIMON TREVOR

My Christian the Lion story

Marc Bolton, September 2011

In early June 2008, someone sent me a link to a YouTube clip. This in itself was nothing extraordinary: I used to get sent YouTube clips all the time and, to be honest, when this one started I didn't hold out much hope. It was silent, grainy and I had no idea what was going on. But for the next few days I couldn't stop thinking about it. A lion padded down a hill, jumped up at two men and started rubbing its head against them like a domestic cat. Why? Who were these men, and why would an apparently wild lion react in such an affectionate way? It definitely warranted further investigation.

The clip was called 'Christian the Lion – Reunion!' I Googled it and found an article at the Daily Mail Online *called 'Christian, the lion who lived in my London living room,' by Victoria Moore, dated 4th May 2007. It told the amazing story of Christian's life – bought from Harrod's by two young men, John Rendall and Ace Bourke (Berg in the article), raised in Chelsea and, after a chance meeting with Bill Travers, returned to the wilds of Africa. Then it told of the later reunion, and how Christian remembered the two men. I realised that this was the footage I'd seen in the clip.*

The more I read, the more I thought that this was a story that needed telling. The article said that Christian's return to the wild was 'funded by a TV programme', so I decided to see whether I could find

that programm. After a bit more Googling, I found the film Christian – the Lion at World's End. Armed with my newly acquired DVD, I set about editing a short video telling Christian's story.

I loved the shots of him playing football in the gardens, so that definitely had to go in. Then all that seemed necessary was the reunion footage. Once I'd got the clips sorted, I wrote some text so people could appreciate the story and understand the significance of what they were watching: a lion remembering its friends after spending a year in the wild.

Now all that was left was the music. In hindsight, it's this that helped to give the video its worldwide appeal. I wish I could say that I thought long and hard about which track to use, but the truth is it came to me straight away. The video was about love and never forgetting, and Whitney Houston's I Will Always Love You (originally written and recorded by Dolly Parton) just seemed perfect. Plus, it was guaranteed to make me cry and for this story I didn't think that was a bad thing. I wanted the song's crescendo to come when Christian jumped up for the first time, so I used that as my starting point and worked backwards. Once the song fitted, I noticed that the clip didn't really have an ending, so I thought about what it meant to me and added a message about love and friendship and getting back in touch with people. That done, I posted it and went to bed.

The next six months were absolutely incredible. The video went from zero views to one million views in less than a month. Soon it was being shown on TV and news shows all over the world. It was being discussed on The View with Whoopi Goldberg, CBS, NBC, London News and Richard and Judy, and receiving its own show on Animal Planet. Before long it had ten million views and John and Ace had been brought together for an interview in Sydney – all because of the little video I made on a laptop in my bedroom. Amazing!

By the end of the year it had been voted Animal Planet's number one video in their 'The Year in Animals', number three on MSNBC's 'Top Ten Viral Videos of 2008' and had been included in YouTube's 'Best of 2008' videos. Virginia McKenna of The Born Free Foundation had done an interview with her son Will Travers discussing the Christian the Lion phenomenon (and very kindly mentioning me by name) and the story had been chosen by Channel Five for an hour-long documentary entitled The Lion from Harrods. Approaching twenty-two million views, the Christian snowball seemed unstoppable.

That was until I returned from working overseas to find a number of emails from YouTube warning that unless I removed the large number of movie clips on my channel, they would delete my entire account. Something about copyright infringement on a massive scale. Unfortunately, I read the emails too late and when I went to my channel to amend the offending videos, everything was gone – including the Christian the Lion video and its multi-million views. Many emails to YouTube followed but not one received a response. To add insult to injury, a few weeks later YouTube contacted me to ask whether my video could be included in a compilation of YouTube's best ever videos. Unsurprisingly, I said no. They used it anyway.

During the video's meteoric rise, I received many emails from people all over the world telling me how much the message had meant to them and that Christian's undying love inspired them on a daily basis. I'd emailed the video to numerous churches around the world – the 'Get back in touch with someone' message had been interpreted as meaning a rediscovery of God – and had received thousands of messages of thanks from people who'd been inspired by the lion's story.

So, there we are: from zero to hero and back to zero in just six months. I reposted the video early in 2009 [http://www.youtube.com/watch?v=md2CW4qp9e8] and finally managed to correct Ace's name from Berg to Bourke (Never use only one *source when researching a video!) The great thing is that thanks to my little video, I've got a fantastic amount of memories – numerous clips from TV shows around the world, the knowledge that I've made people feel happy all over the planet. Best of all, a few weeks ago, I met John Rendall himself and walked with him in the Moravian Close, where he and Christian played forty years ago. Long live the internet!*

LIONS IN TROUBLE

In 1969, when we took Christian to Kenya, there were an estimated four hundred thousand wild lions in Africa. As this book goes to press in 2018, there are probably fewer than twenty thousand. In less than fifty years, the lion population has plummeted by more than ninety per cent.

What's more, in 1969, lion populations were thriving all over Africa. Today there are sustainable populations in only six countries: Kenya, Tanzania, Botswana, Namibia, Zambia and South Africa. The West African lion is presumed extinct. And it is now highly unlikely that sustainable lion populations remain in Somalia, Chad, the Central African Republic, Sudan or the Democratic Republic of the Congo.

A combination of factors has brought about this catastrophe. Civil conflict, expanding human populations and uncontrolled trophy hunting have all played their part. As has habitat loss and destruction, through over-grazing and loss of natural prey. When indigenous herbivores disappear, lions are forced to attack domestic cattle. The reaction is swift: shooting or poisoning. Today the American poison Furadin is easily available all over Africa. Originally manufactured and imported to kill ticks on camels, its alternative use as a baiting poison has been readily exploited, with disastrous repercussions. Furadin in the food chain devastates not only lion populations, but also those of vultures, hyenas, jackals and all the other scavengers, without which carcasses are left to rot and spread disease.

Other diseases also take a toll. In South Africa's Kruger National Park, lions have contracted bovine TB from buffalo, which pick up the infection from domestic cattle when roaming into Mozambique. A weakened buffalo is a prime target for lions, and of course the alpha male takes the choice bits – the heart and liver – where the disease is concentrated. With the death of alpha males, younger inexperienced males are prematurely 'promoted' to head of the pride, with disastrous results. A mature male knows that killing cattle leads to trouble, but 'teenage' lions, which George always said were the hardest to work with, don't know the rules and can cause real problems with domestic stock and sometimes even people.

Prince William's position as patron of Tusk, a conservation organization founded in 1990 and now working in nineteen African countries, has helped draw much-needed worldwide attention to the plight of Africa's rhino and elephant. But we shouldn't overlook the fact that lions are also in serious trouble: indeed, white rhinos, with a population estimated at around twenty thousand, may now be more numerous than lions. When George Adamson was criticised for keeping his focus on lions, he always maintained that a healthy lion population meant healthy wildlife in general. He explained that if lions are well-fed then there must be plentiful prey and thus a thriving environment for the numerous other creatures that make up the ecosystem.

Today, rhino are safe only where high security is in place, such as at the Lewa Wildlife Conservancy in Laikipia, where Anna Mertz persuaded the Craig family to convert their cattle farming land into a rhino conservancy, or at Solio, near Nanyuki, and in the dedicated rhino sanctuary in Meru National Park. Of course they are also safe at Mkomazi, the George Adamson Trust base in Tanzania. Even in these pockets of safety, poaching still persists. The concept of such fenced areas for lions would have so saddened George Adamson, but it appears that this may be the only solution if Christian's descendants are to survive. I remain optimistic. Hopefully, Christian's legacy will raise awareness of the threat to all wildlife. As Tony Fitzjohn wrote: 'We all have a lot to thank Christian for'.

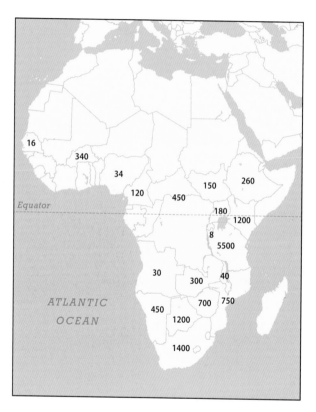

The two maps above illustrate the status of the African lion according to the latest data provided by conservation organisation LionAid (*https://lionaid.org*). Left: estimated African lion populations by country, 2018; right: the distribution of the African lion in 2018 (dark green) compared with the distribution in 1918 (light green) © d-maps.com

ACKNOWLEDGEMENTS

London, 1969 Firstly, of course, Anthony ('Ace') Bourke, my co-guardian of Christian, without whose input of time and love it would have been impossible to raise him. At Harrods Zoo: head buyer Roy Hazle, assistant buyer Sandy Lloyd and long-term staff member Rita Stratta, who entrusted us with Christian's future. At Sophistocat Pine furniture shop: Jennifer-Mary Taylor, Christian's much loved surrogate mother; Joe Harding and John Barnardiston, the shop's co-owners, who so generously allowed Christian to live with us there; Kay Dew, our daily help, who was totally unfazed by having a lion under her feet and vacuum cleaner; Unity Bevis, Christian's best friend, who came to play with him every day; the late Rod and Joan Thomas, who lived in the Moravian Close and introduced us to the Reverend Rex Williamson – who, in turn, allowed us to exercise Christian in the Close; all our neighbours in the World's End, Chelsea, who took Christian to their hearts; Dr Keith Butt, Christian's vet; and Bill Travers and Virginia McKenna, who introduced us to George Adamson and thus paved the way for Christian's rehabilitation in Kenya.

Kenya, 1970 George Adamson, without whose vision and skills Christian could never have been returned to the wild; the Kenya Ministry of Wildlife and Tourism, who agreed to Christian's rehabilitation at Kora; The Tana River Council, the administration headquarters responsible for what was then Kora Reserve; Monty Ruben from Express Transport, who solved so many early logistical problems; George's friend Nevil Baxendale, who built the half-way camp between Nairobi and Kora; Nevil's son Johnny Baxendale (George's former assistant); Stanley Murithii, George's then assistant (who, tragically, died in the course of his work); Terence Adamson, George's brother, who prepared Kora for Christian's arrival, and built Kampi ya Simba; Ken Smith, Provincial Game Warden of Garissa.

In Nairobi, for their generous hospitality: Agneta von Rosen and her late husband Count P A von Rosen; Terri and the late Nick Stobbs; the late Jack and Doria Block; and Ulf and Marianne Aschan; and, for the wonderful welcoming service at Bobby's Bistro in Nairobi, Peter Ngerogoe, described by then Travel Editor of *Tatler* Victoria Mather as 'the best damned head waiter south of the Equator'.

Kenya, from 1971 Tony Fitzjohn, George's assistant, who came to love Christian as much as Ace and I did and was integral to his successful rehabilitation. Christian's relationship with Tony was the cornerstone of Tony's future success in conservation: in 1988, he founded the George Adamson Wildlife Preservation Trust and was deservedly awarded an OBE in 2007 for his services to conservation. Also, Simon Trevor for his superb camera work in capturing the reunion with Christian; Leila Trevor and Dr Sue Haarthorn, who tended Boy – and later Christian – after attacks by wild lions at Kora; and Hamisi Farah, George's loyal cook.

George Adamson Wildlife Preservation Trust (*www.georgeadamson.org*) Founding Chairman the late Dr Keith Eltringham, who steered the charity so wisely during its formative years; Bob Marshall Andrews QC, former MP, who has so eloquently taken on Keith's mantle; Treasurer Andy Mortimer and his late wife Georgina, who was the Trust's incredibly patient and efficient administrator; and my fellow Trustees, Paul Chauveau, Brian Jackman, Anthony Marrian, Tim Peet, Alan Toulson and Peter Wakeman. We're also grateful for the support of Jill Marshall Andrews, Sarah Toulson, Felicity Marrian and Melanie Rendall, and the many long-standing, generous and loyal Friends of Mkomazi. And thanks to the enthusiastic young Junior Committee; Astrid Harbord, Jake Thompson and Henry Morely.

America (*www.wildlifenow.com*) Jeff Stein, Moritz Borman and Ali McGraw at the Tony Fitzjohn/George Adamson Wildlife Trust; Peter Morton; Eli Weis at the WildiZe Foundation (www.wildize.org); Laura Utley, Patricia Sherman, Jorie Butler Kent (founder) and Geoffrey Kent at Friends of Conservation (www.friendsofconservation.org); Reute Butler, Manuela Hung, Muffi Hiss, John Morris and Luzann Fernandez.

Australia Larry Vogelnest, Senior Veterinarian at Taronga Zoo, who visited George Adamson at Kora; Guy Cooper, former Director and Chief Executive of Taronga Conservation Society; Cameron Kerr, current Director and Chief Executive at Taronga Zoological Society; the Taronga Conservation Society's research team at Western Plains Zoo, Dubbo: Rebel Penfold-Russell, Stuart Quin, Robbie Henderson; Candy Reynolds and Judy Crawford (Christian's honorary 'aunts' when in London); Ace's agent Lauren Miller.

Holland Dr Aart Visee, African Wild Dog Foundation; Ted van Dam, and the Suzuki Rhino Club.

South Africa The late Max Borkum, who introduced me to Nelson Mandela: the former president was enthusiastic about the George Adamson Trust's plans for the rehabilitation of black rhinos from South Africa to Mkomazi; the late Jean Borkum; my South African 'sisters,' Shelley and Daphne Borkum. Also, for their generous hospitality over many years: Cally Hotson and her late parents John and Linda Newman; Dita Newman, Jan and Karen Newman and Binky Newman; Morne and Jenny Du Plessis; Pippa Uphill-Brown and the late Geoffrey Uphill-Brown; Cilla Higham; Phil and Liz Biden, owners of Royal Malawane Lodge in Kruger National Park; Johann and Gaynor Rupert; The Hon Pat Cavendish O'Neill (author of *A Lion in the Bedroom*); Marianne Fassler and Charles Botner; Kevin and Mandy Richardson, and the late Roger and Lisa Bury, and Nick and Sandy Magni, in Johannesburg.

Mkomazi National Park, Tanzania Field Director Tony Fitzjohn, who has so successfully perpetuated George Adamson's vision for conservation, and his wife Lucy Fitzjohn, who deals with the endless administration demands of government and benefactors, while finding time to raise four fine young Fitzjohns. Also, Operations Manager Elisaria Nnko, Rhino Sanctuary Manager Semu Pallangyo, Rhino Security Manager Philbert Shindano, Head Rhino tracker Evans Goodluck, Head Dog Keeper Sangito Lema, Workshop Manager Fred Ayo, Dickson Laaya and all Mkomazi's other dedicated staff; Dr Peter Morkel, Field and Veterinary Adviser who has overseen all rhino translocations. Also, The Wildlife Preservation Trust Fund, including founding Chairman Brigadier General Hashim I Mbita, current Chairman Bernard Mchomvu, Charles and Annette Dobie, and Rose Lagemba MP; Tanzania National Parks (TANAPA).

Supporters of the George Adamson Wildlife Preservation Trust
Patron HRH Princess Michael of Kent and HRH Prince Michael of Kent; at the TUSK Trust (*www.tusk. org*), the staff, appeals committee and patrons, including HRH The Duke of Cambridge; the Duchess of Cambridge; the Hon. Life President Sir Christopher Lever Bt.; Chief Executive Charlie Mayhew OBE; HRH Prince Harry, who has visited Mkomazi and contributed to a promotional film. Suzuki Rhino Club and Ted van Dam in Holland for their continued financial support for Mkomazi; Chester Zoo, which donated the Environmental Education bus for the Mkomazi Outreach programme; Lord and Lady Bamford, for their continued generous donation of JCB equipment and spares; artists/adventurers Ollie Williams and Suzi Winstanley (*olliesuzi.com*); Lord Anthony Rufus Isaacs, staunch supporter in both the US and the UK; Venessa Cowham; Damien Aspinall and the Aspinall Foundation; Berry White from Port Lymphe; George Duffield; DHL; at Save the Rhino (*www. savetherhino.org*): Director Cathy Dean; Founding Directors Johnny Roberts and David Stirling; Chairman Tom Kenyon-Slaney.

Christian's legacy
Richard Painter (*www. christianthelionprints.com*) for his fastidious restoration of the photographs in this book; Steve Miller, former volunteer archivist of the Elsa Conservation Trust, who visited Christian at Sophistocat when a pupil at the College of St. Mark and St. John, Chelsea; Jennifer Ratcliff, dedicated former Director of Elsa Ltd in Kenya; Jean Aucutt from the UK Elsa Conservation Trust (www.elsatrust.uk); the late Juanita Carberry, author of *Child of Happy Valley*; Will Travers and Virginia McKenna from the Born Free Foundation (*www.bornfree.org.uk*); Chris McSween and Dr Pieter Kat of LionAid (*www.lionaid.org*), who so generously shared their research with me; Chrysee Bradley Martin, who made such an effort to trace Christian's DNA to the cub Richard (later renamed Godfrey) at Nairobi Orphanage; the late Esmond Bradley Martin; Christian Stebel from Yellow Wing Air Services Ltd (*www.yellowwings.com*), for his many safe landings at Kora; Carol Strebel; Mike and Diane Prettejohn, who kindly lent me their guest cottage at Labarra Ranch in the Sangare Conservancy near Nanyuki, where I finished this book; their supportive neighbours Horace and Linda Burnett, Henry and Jessica Henley, Geordie and Felicia Church, and Janie Collie; the Earl and Countess Enniskillen; Stefano Cheli and Liz Peacock, whose company Cheli & Peacock have so generously hosted me at their lodges (Elsa's Kopje in Meru National Park, Joy's Camp in Shaba National Park, Lewa Safari Camp at Laikipia and Elephant Pepper Camp in the Maasai Mara); and the then managers of those lodges, Philip and Charlie Mason; Richard Mogoro, the former Head Guide at Elsa's Kopje who rescued the cub 'Richard'; Willem and Francien Dolleman; Vanessa Hanka and Marcus Newton; Ava Paton, now manager of Solio Game Ranch in Laikipia; Callum and Sophie McFarlane, now managers at Lewa House; Stephen and Tania Hitchens, partners in Cheli & Peacock; David and Cissy Walker at Sirikoi in the Lewa Wildlfe Conservancy; Ian and Jane Craig, at Lewa; Sue Roberts and the late Willie Roberts, also at Lewa; Stefanie Powers at the William Holden Foundation at the Mount Kenya Safari Club; Donna Hurt; and Ralph and Sussie Helfer, who live in the grounds of the Mount Kenya Safari Club.

SELECTED BIBLIOGRAPHY

Adamson, George. *Bwana Game: The Life Story of George Adamson*. Collins and Harvill Press, 1968.

Adamson, George. *My Pride and Joy*. Collins & Harvill Press,1986. George's autobiographical masterpiece, written after Joy's death.

Adamson, Joy. *Born Free*. First published Collins & Harvill Press, 1960; 50th anniversary edition published by Macmillan, 2010, with foreword by John Rendall.

Adamson, Joy. *Living Free*. Collins & Harvill, 1961. The continued story of Elsa and her cubs.

Adamson, Joy. *Forever Free, Elsa's Pride*. Collins & Harvill Press, London, 1962. Final book in the Elsa trilogy.

Adamson, Joy. *Queen of Shaba: The story of an African Leopard*. The Harvill Press, first edition 1980. Joy's account of rehabilitating a leopard called Penny in Shaba National Park.

Adamson, Joy. *The Searching Spirit*. Collins & Harvill Press, 1978. Joy's autobiography, with a foreword by Elspeth Huxley.

Bourke, Anthony and Rendall, John. *A Lion Called Christian*. First published by William Collins, 1971. Bantam revised edition, 2010.

Cass, Caroline. *Behind the Mask*. Weidenfeld and Nicholson, 1992. A probing biography of Joy Adamson that explains much of her behaviour.

Couffer, Jack. *The Lions of Living Free*. Collins, 1966. The director's frank account of the failure of a sequel to the film *Born Free*. Collins & Harvill Press, 1972.

Fitzjohn, Tony, with Miles Bredin. *Born Wild*. Viking, 2010. The autobiography of George Adamson's Assistant and Field Director of the George Adamson Wildlife Preservation Trust.

Filmography

A Lion called Christian. Beckmann Communications, 1971. Directed by James Hill with cameraman Simon Trevor. Includes the emotive footage of Christian's reunion with John and Ace after his first year in the wild.

Elsa the Lioness. BBC, 1960. David Attenborough's interview with George and Joy Adamson, filmed just before Elsa's death, in which Attenborough coined the phrase: 'a lioness of two worlds'.

Born Free. Columbia Pictures, 1966. Directed by James Hill, produced by Carl Foreman and starring Virginia McKenna as Joy Adamson and Bill Travers as George Adamson. This romanticised account of Joy and George's life with Elsa became a popular classic and deservedly won a Best Music Oscar for John Barry's haunting theme.

The Lion at World's End. Morningstar Productions, 1970. Directed by James Hill. Original version of the documentary account of Christian's life in Chelsea with John and Ace, and his transition from the King's Road to Kora Game Reserve in Kenya.

Living Free. Columbia Pictures, 1972. Directed by Jack Couffer, with Susan Hampshire as Joy and Nigel Davenport as George. Failed to repeat the success of *Born Free*. Neither George nor Joy would assist in the production, following the decision by Carl Foreman and Columbia to sell the lions used in *Born Free*.

The Joy Adamson Story. BBC, 1980. TV documentary written and directed by Dick Thomsett.

Lord of the Lions. Yorkshire Television, 1989. Presented by Sandy Gaul, who interviewed George Adamson a few months before his murder at Kora in 1989.

George Adamson's Funeral. Beerdigung, 1989. News report of George Adamson's funeral. In his eulogy, Richard Leakey gave a clear warning that poaching would no longer be tolerated in the newly upgraded Kora National Reserve, which Leakey acknowledged would never have been established had it not been for Christian.

Reputations: The Joy Adamson Story. BBC, 1996. Produced and directed by Liz Hartford. TV documentary that critically reviewed Joy's Adamson's life and work.

To Walk With Lions. Mosaic Entertainment, 1999. Directed by Carl Schultz. Richard Harris and Honor Blackman were perfectly cast as George and Joy Adamson in this unsentimental biopic of George's assistant Tony Fitzjohn, played by John Mickie. A much under-rated film, in which Harris is superb as George.

Mkomazi: Return of the Rhino. HIT Entertainment, 2000. Produced by Carl Hall with Executive Producer, John Rendall. An account of the arrival from Addo Elephant National Park, South Africa, of the first black rhinos at Mkomazi Reserve, Tanzania, administered by the George Adamson Wildlife Preservation Trust. The calm tones of narrator Edward Fox balance the drama of the rhinos' arrival and their subsequent survival tribulations.

The Lion Cub from Harrods. Blink Films, 2009. Directed by Jackie Osei Tutu. Made-for-TV documentary about the explosion in public awareness of Christian's story following the 2008 posting of the reunion clip, filmed one year after he had started living in the wild.

The Born Free Legacy. Icon Films, 2010. Documentary to mark the 50th anniversary of the publication of *Born Free*.

Elsa: The Lioness that changed the World. BBC Natural History Unit, 2010. Producer, Sacha Mirzoeff; Executive Producer, Brian Leith. Well-researched documentary that uses historic footage of George and Joy with Elsa, and George with Christian.

ABOUT THE AUTHORS

John Rendall is a sixth generation Australian who first came to the UK in 1969. His world trip stalled when he purchased the lion cub Christian from Harrods and, with fellow Australian Anthony (Ace) Bourke, raised him in the King's Road, Chelsea, at the height of 'swinging London'. The opportunity to return Christian to Africa was irresistible, and John and Ace accepted the offer of George Adamson (of *Born Free* legend) to rehabilitate Christian. John has since remained involved with wildlife conservation, helping found the George Adamson Wildlife Preservation Trust, which today manages Kora National Park in Kenya and Mkomazi National Park in Tanzania, and becoming a patron of LionAid. He is still based in Chelsea but regularly escorts groups to Kenya, on the 'Adamson Trail', and more recently to India to see tigers. John's three children have always supported his commitment to conservation, regularly travelling to Africa with him.

Derek Cattani is a London-based award-winning photographer, with a career spanning over forty years. His photographs, covering famous public figures and major world events, have appeared in the *Sunday Times, Daily Mail* and other leading publications. While taking the portrait of the Queen was a career highlight, it was an inauspicious meeting with two young Australians – John Rendall and Ace Bourke – at a swinging Chelsea party in 1970, that would change his life, as he began documenting the story of their unique pet, Christian the lion. After being accepted into Christian's 'human pride,' Derek documented Christian's story, from his early life along the King's Road to his final adventures with the boys in Africa, as he was rehabilitated back into the wild under the expert care of George Adamson.